To: Grandad

Merry Christmas and happy
New Year.

Love and Kisses

Kirsty

X mas 2003

TO SHOOT HARD LABOUR

The Life and Times of Samuel Smith
an Antiguan Workingman
1877-1982

●

Keithlyn B. Smith
Fernando C. Smith

To Shoot Hard Labour:
The Life and times of Samuel Smith
an Antiguan Workingman 1877–1982

First published in 1986 by Edan's Publishers, Toronto Canada

First European Edition by Karia Press in 1989
Copyright © Keithlyn B. Smith and Fernando C. Smith

Cover painting by Mary Anne Tell
Title page illustration and illustration of St. John's, Antigua by
Stephanie Martin
Photographs by Egbert Twaites

ISBN 0 946918 75 9 Pb
ISBN 0 946918 76 7 Hb

KARIA PRESS
41 Rheola Close
London N.17 9TR
U.K.

Printed in Great Britain by
Billing & Sons Ltd, Worcester

TO OUR PARENTS

and

In memory of our grandfather,
MR. SAMUEL PAPA SAMMY SMITH,
whose experience, intellect and strength
made possible this book.

Acknowledgements

Several individuals helped us complete this book. First, and most important we must say thanks to our late grandfather Samuel Smith, who gave unselfishly of his time and energy to make this book a reality. Thanks also to Leone Carr, Brenda Brown, Helen James, Lucein Millette Gomes and Sylvia Philip, all of whom have helped at different times to type the many versions of the original manuscript; and George Barriero who worked on the final product of the manuscript for publication. We are grateful to Egbert Twaites for taking the pictures, and to Sandra Sylvester, Clifton Joseph and Naomi Smith for proofreading the final manuscript.

It is not possible to list the names of the many friends who supported us throughout this project, however we wish to acknowledge the encouragement we received from Al Francis, Glentis Goodwin, Enid Goodwin, Lesroy Merchant, Ernie Letbey, and the late Emile Pigott.

We would also like to acknowledge with affection and gratitude the assistance we received from Patricia K. Murphy.

She made a tremendous contribution to this project. In addition to providing editorial assistance she also provided important creative advice. Also her insights and sensitivity did much to enhance our efforts in making this book a reality.

Special thanks to Carl E. James who over the past years provided advice and encouragement. His continuous interest in this project is reflected in his Foreword. We are particularly grateful to him for his contribution.

Our families are by no means the least among the persons who provided the support and encouragement that kept us persevering. We wish to thank them for their patience and tolerance. Specifically, thanks to Althier Smith and Jeanette Smith, who transcribed the audiotaped interviews. And of course we must mention our wives, Evelyn and Naomi who provided much needed emotional support. They have been patient and understanding with us on the many occasions when we had to be away from home and during those times when we had to spend many hours working on this project.

Finally, to all the other friends and relatives who believed in the possibility and potential of this project, thank you.

Table of Contents

Foreword

I first met Fernando (Ferdie) Smith in Toronto about ten years ago. During one of our many conversations at that time he told me of his paternal grandfather, Samuel Smith, who was then in his late nineties. Ferdie talked of interviewing his grandfather in order to eventually write a book about his life. I was intrigued; not many people have such longevity and, having grown up and completed my early schooling in Antigua, I wanted to know more about the island's history. I felt that my knowledge of the island was somewhat limited, but could not quite say exactly how it was limited.

Over the years I remained impressed with Ferdie's and his brother Keithlyn's dedication and persistence and was convinced that Samuel (Papa Sammy) Smith's story would shed light on parts of the island's history which had remained untold. For me, like other West Indians who went to school before 1975, history was written and taught from what was basically a European perspective, with nothing of the intimate local knowledge that Papa Sammy's accounts provide.

When I saw Keithlyn's original transcripts of the interviews I was fascinated. For the first time I was able to read about local issues and about situations which before remained oral accounts of history; accounts which no doubt reveal the rich and inspiring history of the island.

Spanning as it does the days of slavery in Antigua up to contemporary society and its issues, Papa Sammy's story makes the link between our past and our present. In telling us the stories of his family's life under the brutal conditions of slavery, Papa Sammy speaks of the determined spirit which has made our people survive. Most important is we have known all along, but hardly featured in European versions of Antigua's history: the determination with which Antiguans sought to escape slavery, poverty and exploitation which they resisted and still resist through workers' strikes and other actions.

When we read Papa Sammy's story we read far more than the life of one Antiguan man and his family. We read about ourselves and how strong men and women have been shaped by, and helped to shape Antigua. Indeed, history is not only forged by battles and treaties; it is also, and more importantly, made by the everyday lives of the people, for it is out of this that we get our identity, character and culture.

In contrast, the history we learned in school told only of the West Indies as seen through the eyes of travellers and colonial settlers. But, as Ferdie and Keithlyn show us, our history was not just the little that was recorded in the diaries of governors and generals, it also lived on in voices of local people. It is this richness that writers and observers have tended to ignore.

In sharing the memories of an Antiguan workingman, Ferdie and Keithlyn have deepened our understanding of issues and events that are not unique to Antigua. Slavery and post-emancipation injustices have taken place throughout the Caribbean, Latin America and the United States and readers from these places will probably be able to identify with some of these events and issues in this book.

To see this long project come to fruition is to feel relief and gratitude that such a work exists that provides an Antiguan account of the lives of black people in the western world.

CARL E. TONGE JAMES
YORK UNIVERSITY
TORONTO 1985

Introduction

Perhaps the first person to recognize the importance of what Samuel (Papa Sammy) Smith knew was one of his sons, Hilson Smith. At his urging, we sat down to record over one hundred years of Antiguan history from the grand old man, with the knowledge that nowhere else can there be found such a rich account of the daily life of the Antiguan working people.

His story has its beginnings nearly four hundred years before his birth in 1877, with the Spanish conquest of the Americas and the islands of the Caribbean Sea, and the Portuguese slave trade.

While Caribbean and Latin American readers may be generally familiar with the history of the European conquest of the West Indies and the Americas, the colonial period and slavery and the slave trade, perhaps other readers are not.

In order to set the stage for those who may be less familiar with Caribbean history, this introduction gives a brief account of how Antigua — once a stopping off place for the Arawaks and Caribs, two of the first peoples of the Caribbean — came to be colonized and to rely on black labour, for it is then that the story of Antigua's working people begins.

"Who is there who knows not that the Lord gave everything for our use?" wrote Gonzalo Fernandez de Oviedo y Valdes — travelling companion of the first Admiral of the Spanish fleet, Christopher Columbus, and writer on history and the wonders of nature in the Caribbean islands — on the occasion of Columbus' second journey into the Caribbean. The Lord had little to do with the reasons for the voyage, though His name would be repeatedly invoked by the European powers as first the Spanish, then the French, English, Dutch, Portuguese and Germans spread out into the Americas, Africa and Asia.

It was on this second voyage — inspired, wrote Oviedo y Valdes, by the heartfelt wish of the Spanish Crown that "the souls of these Indians would be for the Lord" — that Columbus returned to the island of Hispaniola, now shared by the Dominican Republic and Haiti. And it was sometime in the autumn on his second trip that he landed on and then gave a Spanish name to Antigua.

But Santa Maria de la Antigua, as Columbus called it, had neither the silver the Spanish would later find in Peru, Bolivia and Mexico, nor the abundant rivers of Puerto Rico. Columbus claimed it for the Crown and moved on.

Columbus moved on because he had not succeeded in his first voyage. When Christopher Columbus set sail in the darkness on that first journey nearly five hundred years ago, it was a Friday morning in early August. As he headed down Spain's Rio Saltes and south into the Atlantic towards what we now call the Canary Islands, he was but one of many European adventurers on the trail of new trade routes to the East and the gold and silver needed to fuel growing commerce.[1]

It was a risky business. Sailors were not always eager to venture into what might await them in "the sea of darkness". Nor were overland trekkers always sure of what to expect as they sought a way around the mountains and deserts that lay in the path to the East. Risky, but rewarding, too. When Portuguese explorer Vasco da Gama finally rounded Africa's Cape of Good Hope, sailing onwards until he put anchor at the Indian port of Calicut in 1488, his backers made a profit of six thousand percent.[2]

Despite repeated voyages, Columbus never found another all-water route to the hard-to-come-by goods of the East. The people of his own time mocked him as a failure for never discovering a way around the barrier of the Americas. It was only in the next century, when silver began to flow out of the mines of Peru and Mexico and into the Spanish treasury that his venture began to seem at all worthwhile.

And although the former first admiral of the Spanish fleet faced ridicule in his own time, his travels to the New World would spark a long and bitter struggle over who would rule the new lands and would raise a new question: Who would work them?

Meanwhile, the first peoples of the Caribbean — the Ciboney, the Arawaks and the Caribs — watched the passing ships from the shore, but lived on for a time as they always had, hunting the guinea pig-like agouti and the coneys with bow and arrow, spearing the kingfish and red snapper with bone-tipped reeds from their dugout canoes, planting the cassava to bake on hot stones for bread. Soon they would no longer be "forgotten by God for so many centuries" as Oviedo y Valdes lamented. Shiploads of Spanish and then French colonizers began to drop anchor.

But for the most part, the European powers left the island of Antigua to itself until nearly one hundred and forty years later, when Englishman Thomas Warner, who had earlier established English colonies on St. Kitts and Monsterrat, arrived to establish the first colony in 1632.

Warner and the thousands of colonists who landed after him had come to extend the territory of the English Crown and to reap the fruits of the New World for the empire.

The push to make use of the Caribbean's land and natural resources soon made it clear to the colonizing countries that something would have to be done to make sure there would be a ready supply of workers.

The first slave trade in the Caribbean drew not on Africans but on Arawaks, the people Columbus spoke of as "loving their neighbours as themselves" and as having "the softest, gentlest

speech in the world". But it proved more difficult to enslave the
Caribs. They withdrew far inland and, according to the Arawaks
with whom they had long been at war, had a reputation for
eating human flesh. The Arawaks quickly sickened and died
from overwork, European diseases and too little proper food.
And like their fellows, the Caribs, many Arawaks swallowed the
bitter cassava, or hanged themselves or flung their bodies into
the seas rather than live in slavery.[3]

If the Caribs and Arawaks would not work for the colonists,
who would? In the early 1500s, a New World Spanish priest,
Bartholemew de las Casas, thought he had come up with some
just answers to the questions of who would labour if the first
peoples would not.

One proposal was that Spanish peasants should be given
special help to settle in the colonies. Another solution, and one
that Las Casas would later say he came to regret, was that each
new world settler should be permitted to keep up to twelve
African slaves.[4]

It is thought that some of the first African slaves to reach the
New World came with the Spanish colonial governor Ovando in
1502. But these slaves escaped the plantations and went to join
the first peoples in the mountains, so vexing the governor that he
advised the Crown that no more be sent. He turned out to be
more annoyed, however, by the lack of hands to till the fields and
cook the food, so before much time had passed he changed his
mind and asked for more.

But black slavery — which would in time become the main
way of making sure that the plantations would have a steady
stream of workers — was in the beginning but one of the many
sources of the forced labour that would plough the vast estate
holdings and toil as domestic servants in the great houses.

It was never the case that whites lacked the constitution to
work under the hot plantation sun or that blacks were somehow
more fit for hard physical labour. These were racist justifications
that came well after the fact.

The matter was rather that the officials of the time were
comfortable in the belief that forced labour was not such a bad
thing, merely the necessary lot of some.[5]

Some of the whites who came to work as unfree labour were indentured servants who had signed a contract binding them to work for a certain amount of time in payment for their passage.[6]

Others were the "redemptionists", down and out poor whites who had agreed to pay the ship's captain the costs of their passage within a given time. Those who did not make the payments were seized and sold to the highest bidder.

Yet others were convicts from cities such as Bristol. Frightened by the stern-faced threats of hanging coming from judges and merchants, petty crooks pleaded to be sent to work the plantations.[7] Still others who would receive no pay for their work were poor whites fleeing the lord of the manor, desperate Irish escaping the landlords and even Germans anxious to leave behind the ruins of the Thirty Years War.

As this commerce in people grew, kidnapping became an everyday thing in London and Bristol. Young girls who had been jailed for disorderly conduct were cordially asked to leave for the West Indies and Cromwell sent prisoners to work in the islands. To be sentenced to forced labour in the New World became so much a part of everyday life that people began to speak of someone having been "barbadosed" — sentenced to work in Barbados or one of the other Caribbean colonies.[8]

But if black slavery had nothing to do with who was fit to work in the noonday sun, it had everything to do with putting cotton on the back of Europe, tobacco in its pipe and sweetening the tea and coffee on its table. Just as the numbers of poor whites who could be convinced, tricked or forced into bound labour dwindled, so too did the need to force them to leave England.[9]

The deciding factor, however, was not that white bound labour was troublesome. It just got to be too expensive. For the money needed to buy a white worker for ten years, the plantation owner could buy a black slave for life and own her children in the bargain. There were problems, too, with the pressganging of white labour. (The kidnappers of Africans did not have to face the outraged working people of Bristol and London who were known to throw stones at the sight of a "spirit", a man — usually an upright and well respected citizen, not a ne'er-do-well — who snatched poor whites to send them across the waters.) Thus, in time, the men who once cracked the whip over the backs of petty crooks came to wield it over black slaves.

A sign of the worth of England's Caribbean and mainland colonies can be seen in the trade wars and in the laws passed back in England that forbade the colonists to encourage any industry that could compete with the factories in the home country. What the factories in England could not use would then be re-exported — at a good profit. Thus within less than one hundred years from the signing of the Treaty of Breda in 1667 (granting England rule over Antigua) after the French occupation, the sugar from this tiny island was already playing an important role in English trade. Between 1714 and 1773, the value the sugar and other goods Antigua shipped to England was worth more than three times the value of the products from England's New England colonies.

Who was doing the work to make this possible? A look at the make up of the population in 1774 gives a good indication. Ninety-three and a half percent of Antigua's population in that year — less than forty-one thousand at the time — were black slaves and the percentage of blacks would stay roughly the same.

By the mid-seventeenth century sugar — first brought to the new world by that failed explorer Christopher Columbus — had spread into Antigua and the rest of the Leeward Islands. There were still not enough hands to tend what was becoming the main crop. Ensuring the steady supply of slave labour to the colonies made up a key part of English foreign policy until 1783. Slavery had the backing of the Crown, of ministers of government and members of parliament, of parsons and priests, and of public opinion in general. The few who spoke out against it were largely ignored.

As the eighteenth century came and went it began to cost more to grow sugar in Antigua and England's Caribbean colonies. The planters found it harder and harder to compete for sales, not only to England, the planters' home country, but also to other countries after the sugar was refined in England. In time what was important to the planters began to be of less and less interest in the halls of Westminster and the laws favouring the goods from the colonies began to stir up resentment. By the time the English parliament moved to do away with slavery in 1833-1834, the decline of the colonies had become very sharp indeed.

A good many of the West Indian estates were now deep in debt to bankers and businessmen abroad. Matters got worse as the planters found the English were buying less and less sugar. Planters could not buy if they could not sell so they had fewer goods shipped to the colonies. Prices shot up as the cost of supplies rose. World gluts in sugar, coffee, rum and cocoa meant that the price the planter could demand turned out to be less than what it cost to produce them. Moreover, shipping to England was costly and there were also import taxes to pay.

No longer could the planters keep up the mills and other equipment, feed and house the slaves, fix up the damages wrought by hurricanes and fire. Much needed credit got harder and harder to come by. And although the knowledge was there to refine sugar in the colonies, thus making it more competitive, it was not until 1845 that parliament took the tax off "improved" sugar.

The writing was on the wall. Colonies like Antigua were no longer of first rank importance to a busily industrializing England. As plantation after plantation faced ruin and the international economy went from bad to worse, free labour became cheaper, a way of cutting the losses.

The move towards abolition was also part and parcel of new social theories in Europe where slavery began to be seen as going against Europe's push for science and technology. (It was not wrong, argued some, but it was backward, a sign of weakness.)

Even so, the increasing resistance to slavery as a way of doing business did not mean that respect would come to the slaves. For the colonists the holding of slaves was the way of showing a white's rank in society. Poor whites might never reach high status, but they held firm to the belief that they were better than blacks or creoles. (After all, the colonies had little else to offer them. Nor did many of the whites see themselves as really at home in the colonies. They longed to get back to England and when they could, they did.)

As Papa Sammy's retelling of stories that were handed down

from the days of slavery makes clear, the slaves had never accepted their servitude as the way to salvation nor had they really given in to it, despite the strong beliefs of the slave owners to the contrary. (Indeed, Christianity was not widely encouraged for the slaves and even the Quakers and the Moravians were known to hold slaves.)

Papa Sammy's grandmother, Countis, was the daughter of a former slave. The accounts of estate life passed down to him are powerful testimony to slaves who refused to be insulted and abused by the masters. Individual resistance, however, was invariably met with harsh reprisals which often resulted in the death of the man or woman who fought back.

So great then was the fear of an organized slave uprising that in Antigua in 1702, the penalty for a slave who injured a white was the loss of the nose or any other part of the body. Nevertheless, there are known slave revolts throughout the Caribbean. In 1728 eight rebellious Antiguan slaves were banished to Maryland or sold to anyone who could ship them to the Spanish coasts. In 1736 an Antiguan slave called Count, or Klass as he was also known, led an aborted attempt to blow up Government House during a ball. In 1831, Antiguan slaves rose up again, this time over the shutting down of their Sunday market. (Although the supposed leader was put to death and others flogged and jailed, the planters later set up a market for Saturday.)

The harsh treatment and shockingly poor working conditions for black workers would continue well into the twentieth century. And, as Papa Sammy's eyewitness accounts reveal, even long after slavery ended, for a black worker to insist on his or her rights as a human being would continue to be met with sometimes fatal reprisals.

Nor, as Papa Sammy points out, would the abolition of slavery translate into the freedom to decide the terms of one's everyday life. Just as English politics and a shaky world economy would lead to the end of slavery, so too would these factors be key in putting limits on blacks' freedom even after the Emancipation.

On most of the islands — Antigua was an exception — an

apprenticeship contract[10] meant blacks would be kept tied to the estates for a number of years after the official abolition of slavery. Because former Antiguan slaves were not forced into an apprenticeship — another form of unfree labour — it is tempting to think that the Emancipation brought them freedom. But a constant thread running through Papa Sammy's accounts of working life is the control that white estate owners continued to hold over the personal and working life of the black majority.

Nonetheless, in Antigua the now-freed women like Papa Sammy's great grandmother, Mother Rachel, and her daughters and their male counterparts put everything they had into leaving estate life to set up free villages, despite the fierce opposition from the planters who were loath to see their labour force walk away. (Other former slaves or their descendents would leave for other islands or Central America in search of work.)

Village people had only themselves to count on and so devised ways of helping each other farm, build and furnish houses and tend to the sick. The women healers, or village doctors, as Papa Sammy called them, served generations of Antiguans. No other medical care was available even when Papa Sammy was a young man.

But free land was hard to come by in Antigua and there was not much of it, so most blacks stayed tied one way or another to the big plantations. It was a living, but just barely. The planters at home and their fellows in England held firmly to the belief that working peoples — black or white — should be paid only the absolute minimum to keep them alive and working. Indeed, in 1842, nearly ten years after the Emancipation, the wage paid to a black working on contract was less than what it had cost to feed, clothe and shelter a slave. And, as Papa Sammy saw with his own eyes, despite the Emancipation, working conditions remained virtually the same as they had for his enslaved great grandmother and estate owner brutality continued to be the normal course of events.

So tied were black workers to the plantations that more than sixty years after slavery ended they rarely left the estate grounds. Papa Sammy was nearly twenty-one years old when he first set foot in St. John's. His reminiscences of that city began in the late

1800's and are the only known account of life in the capital as seen through the eyes of a working man.

Nor did an end to slavery mean that blacks would have a say in determining how and by whom the island would be governed. In 1838, when the population of Antigua was around thirty-six thousand people, only three hundred and twenty-three people were allowed to vote.

This then is the stage on which the story of Samuel (Papa Sammy) Smith, Mother Rachel, Harty Bab, All Man Giant, and Missy Byam — but a few of the tens of thousands of people whose hands and backs and minds have built Antigua — unfolds.

His words speak for themselves. We present exactly what he said, in the conviction that his story brings into the sharp light of the present what has otherwise been hidden from history: a detailed account of what it was like to live and work in Antigua under colonial rule.

Notes

1. Goods from the Eastern trade had themselves been bringing in high profits. But the spices and drugs, silks, perfumes and precious stones had to be carried by horseback and muletrain, on camels and the shoulders of men, over thousands of miles, up and down mountains and across deserts, under constant threat of attack. The governments of the day were levying stiff tolls for passage across their soil. But not all of the dangers were on land. Pirates roamed the high seas and the seas themselves boiled up in storms. By the time the goods reached the last port of call and the Venetian merchants who held the monopoly on the Eastern trade had tacked on their cut, the costs were almost too much to bear. The merchants of Spain, England, France and other European countries wanted their slice and began to press for other routes to the East to break the hold of Venice.

2. Vasco da Gama's all-water route would shift the currents of trade as eager men of commerce set up trading companies to seize the new opportunities. And the rewards continued to be high for European men of commerce. So much so that more than a century later English adventurer Henry Hudson was still searching for a new way to the East.

3. The Caribs tried to drive off the invaders, but no sooner had they rid themselves of one set of ships than another would appear. As late as over a century and a half after Columbus claimed Santa Maria de Antigua for Spain and long after Antigua had passed into English hands, the Caribs would still be trying to force the colonists out of the West Indies.

4. Beginning with the Romans and their captives of war, there had long been slave trade along the Mediterranean. By the middle of the fifteenth century, ships flying the Portuguese flag were carrying Africans to Lisbon to be sold as slaves. In the space of less than ten years, almost one thousand Africans would be kidnapped on the Guinea Coast to be auctioned off to estate owners in Portugal and southern Spain or to monied families in the Portuguese capital who wanted slaves as household help. There were some six thousand African slaves in Portugal by 1460. But just as the European powers had been determined to break the monopoly on trade with the East, so too would they move to take a cut of this new branch of trade.

5. In Europe itself, for example, it was a time of brutal treatment for working people, of cruel poor laws and total indifference to widespread poverty by the rising men of commerce and industry. Working people in general were, in the view of England's Burke, but "miserable sheep" and France's Voltaire swore that everything would be lost if the worker should ever find out he had a mind. Given this thinking, it is not surprising that Europeans found it so easy to justify slavery.

6. In England's colony on the new world mainland, Defoe wrote that the white servant girl was a slave. She was not. Although she too lost her freedom, it was for a definite amount of time and her children would not be automatically

bound to work as forced labour. Nor would she ever literally become a piece of real estate like her African sisters, though the rights of women in general would go on being limited for many generations.

7. In the England of the time, there were over three hundred crimes which called for the death penalty, including pocket picking, shop-lifting, horse and sheep stealing and rabbit poaching from a gentleman's estate. What seemed at the time to have been at least a small mercy seems also to have well suited those passing sentence, many of which owned the estates on which these convict labourers would grind out their days. Burning stacks of the landlord's corn, a not unknown protest by angry tenant farmers, or stealing a piece of cloth or killing the landlord's cattle could all result in sentences to the colonies.

8. In 1835, one year after Britain proclaimed the Emancipation Act freeing black slaves, the penalty for trying to organize a trade union in Britain was transportation to the colonies.

9. At the time of the conquest of the New World and for a long time to some, the European governments were of the belief that the more gold and silver in the country's treasury, the richer it would be. Thus in order to hold on to whatever precious metals they already had on hand, governments passed laws forbidding people to take these metals out of the country. Some countries had gold or silver mines within their borders and Spain had its hand on the silver of Peru, Mexico and Bolivia.

In time, European countries that had neither mines at home nor in their colonies came to accept the notion that the way out of a metal-poor treasury lay in changing the terms of trade. If they sold more to other countries than they bought from these same countries, they reasoned, they would be able to insist that the differnce be paid in hard cash, in gold or silver. But, for this new way of going about things to meet with success, they would also have to make some changes in the way things were at home. They would have to push industry over farming because the goods made in the newly growing factories could command higher prices than the food sold to other countries and would also let them buy fewer things abroad. And for this new scheme to work, for them to successfully compete, they reckoned they would have to slash costs as well. Cutting wages would make sure that their costs would be fewer and, as things turned out, would bring an extra benefit. As country people left the land for the promise of a better life in the cities, or were, as in the case of the Irish and others, forced off the land, there would be plenty of people looking for jobs which paid a minimum. Shipping poor white workers off to the colonies worked against the new way of doing business.

There were problems with white bound labour anyway. A white servant could escape and easily blend in with the free white population, a far more difficult task for a new African slave who spoke no English and would stand out because of colour. White servants grew to expect land at the end of the term of servitude, but a black worker could and would be kept off the land for many generations.

10. Under the terms of the Emancipation the children of slaves born after the Act was passed and all slave children under the age of six were freed; but children older than six and their elders had to serve a four year apprenticeship before being freed. This measure did not apply to Antigua; there the slaves were immediately freed.

1
The Family:
Planting Sucker Follow the Root

I have no doubt that my race was brought here from Africa. When it comes to Africa — the mother land — my family could not give me the slightest idea of how life was up there. Absolutely nothing. I was surprised that my family did not know head nor tail of the place where their generations was from. But I can't blame them, for up to today — with all the education — very few people in Antigua know much about Africa. You see, slaves wasn't allowed to know where they come from or even what was the fate of their family on other estates. So I don't know anything about the land of my roots.

I believe that planting sucker follow the root.[1] I wanted to know for sure when my family was brought to the West Indies. I wanted to hear from the horse's mouth how was the journey from Africa to this side of the world,[2] how rough it was, what cause them not to die before they reach here. I wanted to know which island the ship landed first with them; if Antigua was not

1. A belief that family members take after each other, a belief in heredity.
2. To the West Indies.

the first island, where was that? I wanted to know if they were living in another West Indian island before they were shipped to Antigua. I wanted my parents to tell me if they knew anything of the capture, if they knew how did it happen. I wanted to know what my family was like in Africa. I wanted to know from what tribe my family came and if tribal leaders come from my family. After slavery end, almost every Antiguan did not want to hear anything about slavery. Nothing whatsoever. They were ashamed. But I wanted to know.

One of Antigua's big shots, Mr. R.S.D. Goodwin — he was an estate owner and big wheel among the politicians — told me that my people came from the west cost of Africa. Mr. Goodwin was a bright man, but that's all he could tell me. Maybe that's all he knew about any of the slaves — from the west coast — and where, he could not say. I did not even get the feeling that he was sure of what he was saying.

I wanted to know more. I wanted to know if the family had any worthless people in there or any criminals. In my young days, plenty people had cocobay,[3] so I wanted to know if any of my family had that dreadful disease or if any of my family ever was crazy. You know, some diseases run right through families from generation to generation. Also, some people have long livers in they family, others cut off quick.[4] But there was nobody that could give me any clue of what the family root was like.

I know that slavery was terrible, with love ones torn from the mother arms and sold away like animals. It's always been a pain to me to know that white people use to take pleasure in selling human beings some time ago. What a pain to our people.

I know from my old ones that the slaves was locked in for examination when the massa was selling. If there was agreement reached on the ones up for sale, or they decide on the ones up for swap, they would go and the other slaves would just have to miss them. Where they would go was a very big secret that only the slave massas know about. They always use to make sure that the families of the sold negas[5] didn't have any idea of where they was

3. Leprosy.
4. Some families tend to live a long time; others die young.
5. Blacks.

taken. If the family ever harbour the thought of running away to look for them, they would not know where to go. They would have beams[6] to find them; it would be one of the biggest accident if they ever butt up[7] on them.

The way it usually happened was slave owners that lived close together would normally go far away to buy slaves. And slaves of one plantation wasn't allowed to mix with the slaves of another plantation; they worked the plantation and then back to the slave house, lived all their lives, dead and gone and never put foot off[8] the plantation. Only once in a blue moon a slave would attempt to run away. That was like a jail-man trying to escape. In most cases, the jail man would get caught and have to do more time. Not so with a slave. That poor slave would be properly dealt with[9] and maybe that man or woman would die. They never sarbice[10] to themselves afterwards.

My old ones use to tell me that the Antiguan slave massa seldom would sell man slaves. Things would have to be pretty bad with them to sell a young man slave, or big man for that matter. The man slave was to shoot hard labour[11] for the master.

I know from my mother that when slavery end, her great-grandmother Rachael could hardly speak English; she could only mumble a word or two of the language. My mother also said that after slavery end Rachel pick up a few words[12], but nothing much to speak about. This give me the idea that my mother family did not come to the West Indies too long before the bakkra[13] stop bringing slaves. You see, if Rachael was born in Antigua, I think that she would be able to talk the language. So from my own calculation, I reckon that Rachael reach Antigua sometime close to the year 1800.

I do know for sure that Rachael was owned by the Old Road

6. They would need searchlights to find their missing relatives, i.e. it was practically impossible.
7. It would only be by accident that they would come into contact with each other.
8. Never set foot off the plantation, never left it.
9. Be severely punished.
10. They would never fully recover from the blows.
11. To work hard at physical labour.
12. Of English.
13. White plantation owners; by extension whites.

Plantation. She had three gal picknee[14] — Minty, Fanny and Barba.

One day Minty owner went and sold her to another slave massa. Poor Rachael was well shook up, she bawl plenty[15] and so did Fanny and Barba. But slaves have to keep them bawling to themselves. (When a slave disappear, that was that. Massa was the owner and he do what he like for they was his property.) Mother Rachael did not know who it was that bought Minty. She didn't see them, or even what way the slave cart went. That's how it was when Minty was sold and gone away from her people.

Minty was young and did not get to have a child yet. Day in and day out, the family lament over her. But nobody else but she was sold. Emancipation day come and meet the rest of the family living together at Old Road. Then the owners didn't have the headache to provide food for slaves. The slaves do the work in them own garden and feed themselves after slavery end.

The truth is, white massa didn't have much use for old worn-out slaves. The ones that was old and couldn't work hard had to leave the plantation. But not for freedom. No, it was the custom of the Old Road slave massas to take the weak and sick slaves out to sea and throw them overboard. They didn't have any time to dig holes and bury them. I think that everybody in Antigua know the story about a slave that was taken away and bury alive. She was crying, "Massa, me no dead yet! No bury me!" Now massa say, "I have money to buy more, pull um go along."[16]

You know, it's a strange thing, but I heard that when slavery was over the slaves at Old Road didn't even get drunk. I heard there was no great happiness among them. They didn't know what would happen, so them give assurances that they will not leave the plantation, that they will continue on working for the old owners. The old slave massas let them continue to work the ground and grow food for themselves.

But though assurances was given, the young slaves wanted to know what the land was like. So most of the young ones didn't stay at Old Road after slavery end. Some drift from plantation to

14. Children.
15. She wept for a long time.
16. "I have money to buy more, get on with the job of burying her."

plantation; others settle down in one place.

Now the old slave massas at Old Road was tricky and smart people. After slavery end they wanted the strong slaves they sell or swap off during slavery to come back to work on their plantation. Them thought them have proper luck: slavery was all over and they wouldn't even have to buy them back. They would have both the slaves and the money. So the bad-minded slave massas at the Old Road Plantation make sure they tell everybody where their people can be found. All the families say how they give thanks to massa for his great interest, but everybody have in mind not to return to Old Road. People badly want to unite with the family — particularly the womenkind. I hear that the women was furious and desperate to find their people.

That was how Rachael learnt where Minty was for the first time and who bought her. Minty was sold to the Sandersons plantation owners. Rachael could not understand very well what massa was saying so she take her bigger daughter for him to explain about the whereabouts of Minty. Rachael understood then that Minty was at Sandersons Estate, but neither Rachael nor her gals knew where Sandersons was for they never put foot off the Old Road Plantation. But wherever Sandersons was, they was determined to go. Massa, he did not hesitate to explain again and again how they could reach Sandersons. He wanted Minty back; now she was free to work the old estate.

The two sisters, Fanny and Barba, and Mother Rachael got ready to journey to Sandersons in search of Minty. They want a man to follow them, but the man — he was one of the stud or server[17] of the plantation — said no. Still and all, them women was so bound and determined to find Minty only death could stop them. The plan was that they would leave Old Road very early in the morning, when moon carry day.[18] Moonlight must be bright like a goo'back[19] before them leave Old Road. The time come and they start travelling in the north-easterly direction, by

17. A slave used to breed other slaves.
18. At dawn.
19. The Bible: the moon must shine as brightly as the words in the Good Book for them to see the way.

way of Fig Tree Hill, through Follies, then on to All Saints and to Sandersons.

Now Fig Tree Hill be less than a mile from Old Road, but the women never know what that hill was like, for during their entire life as slaves they had never gone that far. That morning, when they set out to find Minty, was the first time they was travelling to Fig Tree Hill, the short way to Sandersons — they was told by massa.

It was not too long before trouble start. Mother Rachael couldn't climb Fig Tree Hill. She had a bad foot and the road was rugged and steep, made up of all flinstones[20] and she was afraid she would fall in the gully. She got all the help and push from Fanny and Barba, but the old lady could not climb that hill. That was bad luck, but old Rachael could not see the way.[21] All the glee suddenly turn into pain.

After staying at the bottom of the hill for some time, they decide pride no feel no pain[22] and they would just have to brave whatever bad luck there was. So they turn back and take another route. There was no suggestion of leaving Rachael behind because them gals love them mother: no search for Minty without Rachael. Anyway, they dine, she go supper.[23]

The very next morning, Rachael, Fanny and Barba set off again in the bright moonlight to go to Sandersons. This time it was the twenty mile journey through Urlings to Bolans and Ottos Estate and then on to Briggins Road, through Freeman's Ville and Sandersons; they did not travel on any part of the road before, neither did they know what the distance was. The road was stony, but with very little hills to climb, no rising of any significance.

Fanny was the leader. When old Rachael wanted a man to follow them and it was taking some time, Fanny say to hell with that, she didn't need any man to follow them. Fanny walk with a

---

20. Small, sharp stones.
21. Rachael knew she would be unable to climb the hill.
22. Pride goes before a fall, i.e., they would have to accept that they could not climb the hill and would have to find another route.
23. They will be together all the time.

old cane bill,[24] naturally, to defend herself and family if attacked. The bundle was light — two roast dumplings, some molasses and a bottle of water and some mangoes. That and them God was all they have.

The journey went fine up to the time they reach a church. Old Rachael was afraid to pass that church for she remembered one Good Friday when she was with some other slaves and they get licks because they linger at the church in Old Road. Rachael wanted them to get off the road. Slavery was just over and fresh in her mind. That place was belonging to massa and she didn't want to get too close.

Anyway, Fanny again drag old Rachael on. She put enough faith in her and they eventually pass the church.

On the way down the road was a large sand-box tree. They decided to take a breeze off[25] under the tree, rest the old lady foot. As soon as they get under the tree, a man approach them, saying that his massa never allow nobody to linger at Yorks[26] them time of day. They quickly move on from under the tree.

As they go on, they begin getting company. It was getting on to morning, so people was travelling to and fro. When them reach Ottos Estate, Fanny and Barba want Rachael to again rest the foot. By daybreak they have full knowledge of the remainder of the journey and exactly where is Sandersons. When they leave Ottos, the road was busy with people travelling up and down. It could have been much more tiresome, but the company on the road and their determination help them to forget the pressure.

By the time it was broad daylight they were making friends. A man follow them past Sea View Farm. This man loved Fanny and promise to check them out at Sandersons. Fanny, Barba and Rachael reach Sandersons early enough that morning, but not before the gangs went out to work the fields. There wasn't many people around the estate-works that could give them news of Minty, but the women were confident that Minty was there so them patiently wait until the gangs finish working at the end of the day.

24. Sharp steel instrument for cutting cane.
25. They decided to rest.
26. No one was allowed on the estates at that time of day.

When that time come they were well-disappointed. The people at Sandersons know Minty, but she was no longer at that plantation. She was sold to the massas at Betty's Hope. On hearing that news, Mother Rachael bust into tears and so did little sister Barba. Them nearly have fit. Would they find Minty after all? It was like Bible days — Rachael wept. Fanny again was the comforter, the person with the heart. Fanny too was well-disappointed, but she was a determined person, not the kind that give up easily. It was night then and they decide to stay over at Sanderson. Them never sleep that night for worry about Minty.

As day clear,[27] they drink some hot water and start the journey to Betty's Hope, not too far away from Sandersons, the distance maybe just three miles. They reach there in quick time, but nobody know anybody by the name of Minty. Frustration was just about to creep in when they see her. Well, them let loose, for God help them find Minty. That was the freedom; only when they find Minty they really believe that slavery was all over for sure. Minty had a brand on she hand. My mother said it was number 104. And that's the number massa know she as. Governor Patrick Ross end the branding of slaves in Antigua in 1828.

Rachael and her daughters, in love and joy, settle in at Betty's Hope. Them wipe foot[28] from Old Road. They hate the old plantation where they used to live. They hate the people that sold them loved one. Old Road with all its plenty food could not behold them again. Even if they did not find Minty, they would not go back to Old Road. They lived at Betty's hope until Rachael die.

Now the living conditions at Betty's Hope was horrible and after the death of Rachael the family went on to live at Vernon's Estate. By then Fanny had a gal-child she call Countis. The family was filled with women. They never told me of any man that was in the family; most of the children didn't know the father. (You see, in them days, a nega man could not count himself as father. The picknee the man make belong to massa.)

27. At daybreak.
28. They left Old Road Plantation.

It was just a few years a-back that nega man get to take on the responsibility of father, so back then nega picknee carry the name of the estate owner. That practice live on a long time after slavery end. People seriously had the feeling that the child belong to the bakkra and the mother would usually take the child to the massa. In most cases, it would be massa that name the baby. The man that was the rightful father couldn't have nothing to do with the child. Many times he would not even know that a particular woman was making a child for him.

Rachael and all her children were jet black. Rachael's first grandchild, Countis, was of a much lighter complexion. It was there at Vernon's that Countis had a gal-child by the name of Margarette. Countis decide to follow the custom at the time. The last name of the chief planter at Vernon's was Edwards, so she call the child Margarette Edwards.

Margarette was the first of us to go to school. She spent three years at a school at Gilberts that was run by a Methodist minister. Now in them days, education was mainly to write your name and sing "God Save the Queen". Maybe also some religious verses were pick up in between.

Times got hard at Vernon's and the houses was in bad condition. The family drift to North Sound in search of a better life. It was there at North Sound that Margarette grew up and went to live common-law with Daniel Smith. Margarette had two gals at North Sound; the first she name after her grandmother Fanny and the second after her great-aunt Minty. The living condition at North Sound was terrible so Margarette and Daniel and them two little gals decide to try it at Jonas Estate.

It was at Jonas Estate in 1877 that Margarette gave birth to her first boy-child, the first man to arrive in the family since the root was pluck up from Africa and brought to the West Indies many generations ago. Happy-go-lucky,[29] the name of the chief planter at Jonas back then was Samuel Smith. My mother and father name that first man picknee after him. Me, Samuel Smith, was that man.

29. As luck would have it, the chief planter's name was Samuel Smith.

That is how, in the name of the Lord, I arrive on Monday, 1st January, New Year's Day 1877 at Jonas Estate to face the world and all it have to offer. My mother, Margarette, was a strong woman; she have eighteen children, the number of men being equal to the women. She had us over a time of twenty-three years, without the help of a nurse. A lot of times, she work up to the last day before the child was born. My father did not know much about his family. He told me that his parents come from the Guinea Coast and that he have relations in Barbuda.

Both Rachael and Fanny die before I was born, but I knew my grandmother, Countis. She use to take care of us so my mother could go to work. For a little more than ten years after I was born, my parents endure the hard life of Jonas Estate.

Sunday, the horse's day off; estate workers took over the pulling of Massa and Missis to church.

2

Estate Life:
Planter Kill King and Rule Country

The northern side of Freeman's Ville was part of Jonas Estate long ago. Jonas wasn't a large estate, but was suppose to be one of the best on the island. It was cut in two by a stream that run off the hill of western All Saints and through Jonas down into the sea at Blackman's Bay. Both sides of that stream was famous for the very rich sugar crop and for the plenty vegetables and fruits.

It was indeed a rich place, but the ex-slaves had nothing. I was born there at Jonas, forty-three years after slavery end, and up to that time, the ex-slaves had nothing.

Take schooling for example, I would say that at least nine out of every ten of our people never put foot in a school door. Bakkra have no interest to see nega people learn to read. And it also seem to me that the English government was very late to do something about the matter.

Some of our people use to go to the schools of the Methodists and the Moravians. Now the Anglicans, they had schools, too, but them schools was for massa's children. And that's the way it was for a long time. As far as bring up[1] picknee goes, it was that the mother drop out[2] the child and as soon as that child was old enough, well the small gang[3] was there waiting. Sometimes the parents would not even know the child's age, but providing that that child look big enough, the parents will tell massa that the child was twelve years old.

Back then, people was hungry for them picknee to reach twelve years or even look like twelve years. They wanted the day to come to get them in the small gangs to help the family. That was the way to survive in them days, so some parents never thought of school.

It seems to me the lack of schooling help to keep us down. Our real school was in the fields. There we learn how to face the dew, the rain and the boiling sun. Them fields also teach us how to use the forks[4], hoes, and cane bills. We use those tools for massa's benefits.

Them force us to have manners.[5] I personally had too much, but somebody with no manners, somebody unruly[6] was gibbetted.[7] Bakkra always say, "Manners maketh the man". Well, let me tell you, not in Antigua, maybe somewhere else, I don't know. It maketh us slaves instead. We suffer privation after slavery because we was dotish,[8] plenty dotish.

From what I know, the life was worse, and that always make me wonder just how was it that the slaves survive.

Whenever there was a fight or quarrel among nega-house people, it would be massa that would decide who was to get punish and how the punishment would be. Some of the times the massa would punish everybody mixed up in it, and rightfully or wrongfully, them all get punish when them ready.[9] But to be driven off the estate was the worst that could happen to you.

1. As far as child-raising was concerned.
2. Gave birth.
3. Child labour.
4. Pitchforks.
5. To be obedient.
6. Rebellious.
7. To be beaten or tortured.
8. Subservient.
9. When the estate owners felt like it.

People would settle for almost anything else — be whipped, be locked up in estate cellar for a time. The least punishment was to get suspended without pay for some time.

Now some people didn't understand the kind of gang-up that took place by the Bakkra against the nega-house people and they believe that to have to leave the estate was the least punishment. But things was not as easy as that. A nega-house man could not live on another estate if he offend even one planter. If one planter tell him to leave, the others would usually refuse to let him work and live on their plantation, and that poor fellow wouldn't have a place to turn to for a long, long time. Dog better than he when that happen.

Estate life get to be too much for us. We couldn't make any noise. Let me put it good: noise couldn't be made within the hearing of the massa, for he would lick everybody, big and little. Nega-house people could not make merry, make massa see or hear. We have to go far from the Buff[10] to make our music for we dare not disturb massa. We at Jonas use to make our music at an old tamarind tree, north of where Freeman's Ville was. That use to be about a mile from Jonas. Now the people over at North Sound would make their music at the Old Pond, a mile or so away from where them live.

The bakkra was hateful to the womenkind. I hear that in the last century it was the general feeling among the bakkra that nega woman was unclean, inferior and taint everlastingly with dirt and filth. But it seem that this belief get even worse when the century end and the women was terribly subject to rape and other things of that kind from the massa and his sons. Many times some planter would rape a mother and her daughters. If the women get pregnant in the event, they dare not tell how it happen. If they somehow be brave enough to tell them family or friend and the news spread, then massa would come down hard on the women, they could even lose them life.

At Jonas Estate there was a nega woman by the name of Missy Byam. She get raped by Massa Ted Cole, one of the English planters on the estate. Missy Byam's big daughter Kate — as it

10. Far from the bluff; estate owners' homes were often built on a bluff, thus the workers had to go far away from where the owner lived in order to play music, etc.

was the custom back then — use to go and work with her mother in order to help out the family. Now Massa Ted Cole already rape Missy Byam. Then he go and rape Kate, just thirteen years old, and get her pregnant. When Cole hear that Kate get pregnant, he threaten her and tell her never to come back to Jonas Estate for he have fear the news would reach the ears of his wife. Now Kate, she was either brave or stupid; she tell her friends about what happen and one of them take the story back to Cole. His pride was severely hurt. He did not want that news to spread, even though such a thing was common on the estates. Massa Cole would definitely get the cold shoulder by his white wife — not for the rape, but for being with a nega gal.

Some time pass and Massa Cole send for Kate and sternly warn her about what he hear. He really chastise Kate to the proper with his tongue and again tell her not to put foot on Jonas.

Kate answer back, something that never happen before. Another woman would just accept what happen and be saddle with a fatherless child. Not Kate. Well Cole took very unkindly to the rudeness of a little nega gal. He immediately let loose his dogs on her. Kate try to escape the beasts and she fall into Works Pond. That pond was deep.

The gang working nearby saw Kate fall into the pond, but they did nothing to save her. They allow her to drown. They have to, or massa would say they betray him and they would pay the penalty for it. Kate could not swim and went under. Massa Cole watch all this with glee and shout, "Give the child to the man under there!" That crime on a poor nega gal mean nothing to the other black workers, so fearful was they of the massa that they dare not speak out.

Kate's body stay there in the pond for some days until it became afloat. She was bury west of Freeman's Ville amongst the graves of her people. Now I ask you, could there be any harder times? For a fact, at one stage, I was feeling that life wasn't worth living. I don't know how I escape that place. I believe God love me for there was nobody who could tell Massa Cole nothing. Planters kill king and rule country.[11]

11. The planters were all-powerful.

I remember how bad was the housing on the estates. When the people find it hard to move from the estates to the villages after slavery end, the houses get to be very over-crowded. At the same time, you couldn't complain over the conditions, for planter say you free to leave: "The freedom that you wait on so long was granted long time ago, the people[12] that were so big and generous to grant that freedom must also provide other things. Why look at us to provide?" was what they would say.

The conditions of the houses rapidly run down after the Emancipation even though they were strongly built. The normal size house was about sixty feet long by forty feet wide and almost all the houses would have cellars. The usual height of the cellars was between three feet to three feet six inches, and the width and length of the cellars was generally that of the house. The cellars was the pillars of the houses and was made up of stones fastened together with white lime. The sill would be made of wood that was five inches by five inches or six by six. The window side would be covered by board and shingles. The other sides would be of board only. The roofs too was covered with shingles and sometimes felt would be used. The houses was also strengthen by several upright posts but there were no partitions.

Most of the houses were leak. We use to put in old cloth or trash to cork the holes. If the holes was large we would plait the trash before we forced it in — that provide some grip — and the plug would not be force out that easy by hard wind. Since it was impossible for anybody to cork all the holes of the houses, we would only cork the big ones and leave the smaller holes to whistle when the wind would blow. So after a time we would generally get wet when it rain. We would just have to face the discomfort. As a matter of fact, we got use to it. Only now, I can say it was hell, living hell and more than that.

Neither were there screens in the houses. Nothing to separate one family from the other. We use to live together like a flock of cattle, like goats or sheep in a pen. The truth is, there was no difference to speak of between the life of the animals and ours.

Try and understand, there was very little repairs done to them houses. When the floor start to rotten, the people living there

12. The English parliament which legislated the abolition of slavery.

would pluck up the floor — the whole thing — to keep themselves from falling in the cellar. The drop to the cellar would be about three and half feet and many children would get hurt that way when the floor was not pluck up. When the floor get pluck up, the bottom of the cellar would be the floor of the house. The bottom was earth.

Now that earth was generally full of jiggers.[13] Nearly all the nega-house people would have that disease for the nega house and them full of jigger foot since the jigger get into the feet of the person and keep them from walking properly. But if you was smart enough to wash your feet with a little carbolic water now and again you would not get jigger foot.

Rats, mice, spiders, centipedes, scorpions and other creatures also lived in the houses. It seems as if them creatures had the belief that the houses was theirs and we had no right in them. The rats in particular was fierce. Now the other creatures would run when people go and attack them, but them rats would generally return the attack; they would jump at their offenders with serious efforts to bite them. Rats even almost take over the houses at nights. Them bite anything and everybody. Sometimes they would get so bad in the houses that you would have to wrap up your feet at nights. Babies could not be left alone and bigger children would sometimes just have to get out of the way of the rats and let them escape.

Scorpions and centipedes also would terrorize our people. They would crawl about real quiet, hardly make a stir. They always seem to have the art of not giving any idea that they was around and would smartly lurk around in our clothes or on our lodgings. Quite often we only would happen to see them when they had already bit us. The sting was sometimes deadly. Now we wanted to make smoke to keep them out of the houses, even for a little while at nights, but massa have the last say on making fire. Sometimes he say yes and sometimes no.

Nega-house people knew nothing call privacy. Good or bad was practiced openly. Picknee could not escape the open vice and we could do nothing to change the way things was. What could them do? Nothing. Not a Jesus thing. Some parents

13. Mite larva which becomes attached to the skin.

wanted to keep their children away from the vices, but that was impossible — so a young gal usually start to have children at age thirteen in them days. It was unusual for a woman to start having children at twenty-one or so. The gal and them hardly get to grow up.

Not only was the houses bad, there was no sanitation to speak of. There was no soap, neither was there disinfectants of any kind. My mother use to wash our skin with light carbolic water to keep the lice and fleas off our bodies. Most nega-house people hardly had regular baths so there was a constant build up of dirt on the body. Maybe a person wouldn't have a bath for several months. We use to say, "Under you neck can grow potatoes", and that was the usual thing among estate people. Of course, man sweat used to smell high. The truth is, it was terrible, but we have to put up with it for many years. You know, only when a person is out of something that them realize how bad it was. That situation was part of nega-house life — part of us — part of our whole system. If you didn't live in it, you would probably feel it more, but most of us didn't think of the misery we was in.

Back then we didn't think it was funny[14] to have lice. Many people would have more lice than a common dog would have, so you would often see people combing the hair over a piece of cloth. At every stroke of the comb the lice would pour onto the cloth — them drop like falling rain. Still and all, lice bit people any place. They even use to embarrass people in church and at weddings. Even when things was better, you can't dress too well because lice keep on biting you. People would also crush the lice by the fingers or the teeth. I don't know if this was a ritual, but it was the strict custom of estate negas to get rid of the lice that way. The poor people also took pleasure[15] to bite lice — that was how bad things was. I know some people don't think we should talk about such things now, but that's how life was when I was a boy. Back then a louse found in the head of a newly born child was accepted as a sign of the child possessing knowledge.

I remember other filth. Every estate had a kooka bendal in nearby bushes and that kooka bendal was use to dispose of

14. Unusual.
15. Were accustomed.

human waste and other filthy matters. The smell was awful. No one ever even thought to cover the filth. Neither was there any authority to do anything about it. Flies and mosquitos would swarm into the houses from the kooka bendal, they would get in the water we would drink and on our food. The worse thing, though, was when them germ-carrying creatures would get on the old tango — the meat from old dead cattle — or on the fish left to dry in the sun. Plenty times the flies was so plentiful that they would cover the whole piece of tango. Lots of people got sick with all kinds of diseases. Of course we only learnt that was the cause many years afterwards.

Now them cattle was massa's blessed animals for sure. I can't remember them killing any of them for nothing. When cattle couldn't work anymore, the bakkra would let them die naturally. Then the tango would be cut up and share out among nega-house people. But nobody outside the estate could get any of that meat. There was no other meat, so you can figure how quarrel and fight broke out again and again for the tango. Although that meat was tough like hide, it was sumptuous Sunday food or special meal for we. Tango not used was left to dry in the sun for there was no other means of preserving meat.

Clothing was just about as hard to come by as meat. There was hardly any money to buy clothes so we would have to patch them again and again to try and keep them whole. With so many different pieces of cloth it was hard to tell the original colour of the garment after a while. Some people could hardly change their clothes for they would have to wear them nights and days. We were in a state of almost hopelessness, I tell you.

Grownups seldom would have under-clothes. In truth and fact, quite a lot of them didn't know what was called under-clothes. The younger boys would wear a tail shirt — a long collarless shirt, usually of flour bag materials — particularly made to cover the lower part of the body. But you didn't wear it if you had some trousers. Some boys would be eighteen and nineteen years old before they would start to wear trousers. Then, as was the custom, they would tie up the tail in front when they had on the trousers.

We were accustomed to wear dungery trousers along with

flour bag or nankeen shirts. Nankeen materials was the cheapest and they use to give away the flour bags. Later on we used to use this other cheap cloth — blue zepher — to make shirts and that same cloth made the garments for women.

Now massa's clothes was entirely different to ours and made up from different materials. The bakkra generally use to wear black pants and white shirts, or khaki pants and white shirts and sometimes they would wear beige pants and light blue shirts. Massa's old and unwanted clothes was given to them with manners. Well, a lot of planters had big bellies, so their trousers did not fit too well on our people. But even so, if a nega-house man had on massa's clothes, it was "good for them". This mean these people did everything massa want — carry news on one another, make every attempt to stay in massa's good books. Them hand-me-downs or wagy, as we call them, were very well-needed to cover up the nakedness.

In the meanwhile, the planters always regard the reaping of the crop as a very serious matter and it better be reap in quick time too. Both the workers at the mills and the ones in the fields had to shoot hard labour. Particular care was taken during the grinding operations to make sure that the mills was always in operation. Now despite the special efforts to keep them mills turning over without stopping, they would get choked sometimes, mainly from being fed too much sugar cane. Whenever that would happen, the wrath of the planter would come down quick on the worker that get the blame.

At Jonas, the planter in charge of the grinding operations would hardly ever leave the mills. Whenever he would have cause to leave, the chief engineer would come and take charge. Chief planter Samuel Smith got along reasonably good — for the times — with the workers at Jonas and with the people living nearby. From what I hear, Smith was the first English planter that promoted a black man — Casper Thomas of All Saints — to be the assistant millman. Now Casper was a good worker and he knew the operations very well. He was also a blacksmith and he would use his knowledge to fit things together to keep them mills running. You see, back then, the position of assistant millman was seen as a great step forward for the workers. And it was a big thing, although that promotion of Casper's did not mean more pay for him.

Then one day, Planter Smith went back to England and his brother Arthur come out to take his place.

Trouble come with the first crop. Casper Thomas was walking on the millbed when he slipped and his hand get into the working mills. The force of the mills pull him in. The other workers move fast to stop the mills, but nothing could save Casper.

Young Massa Arthur heard the mills stop turning while he was away at lunch. He immediately rush to the mills. On reaching there he saw Casper lying on the ground with the workers all around him. Massa Arthur shout in great anger, "Who the hell told you all to stop my mill!" Nobody had courage to answer. Them rush back to their jobs and the chief engineer start up the mills again. Work continue as though nothing happen. They left the body right there.

Massa Arthur make it clear in his fury that he was not about to lose money for the time the mills was down. After a while he send two workers to take the body away and tell Casper's parents. The estate give the family a coffin and that was that for Casper. At the end of the week, Massa Arthur take out what he claim was a half a day's pay from everybody that work the day Casper die. And what he call "half a day's pay" amount to half of what the workers would usually get for the week.

That bakkra was also quick to use the whip on people. He was one to take pleasure in taking workers before the magistrate. His favourite thing use to be to say, "I'll lick you and the magistrate will jail you". And he could do it, too.

The planters also use to use the militia to keep people in check and the militia would have the back up of the magistrates and the jail-house and the government. No way for us to fight back — it was like worm going against nest of ants — for the bakkra was the militia and the magistrates and the jail-house and the government. Whatever happen to us, we must grunt and bear it. If you didn't have manners, them give you the cat-o-nine and them hang you in jail. Nothing for it. You dead and gone. Them give you coffin and that's that.

Under Massa Arthur they use to wet down the people before

they whip them and then leave them tie to a post for a long time. If you got licks for stealing, you could be tie up to the post overnight.

Not so long after Massa Arthur reach Jonas another planter arrive, Massa Ben. Me no think that anyone who was around at the time could forget them two and the wickedness they have in them and them practice.

Never will I forget what happen at that place with my best friend, Henzel Weatherhead Smith. He was around twelve years older than me, born to Carlos Weatherhead and Fancy Crump. Now Henzel's father Carlos was born on a estate near Old Road to a slave name Missy Tom. When Carlos was about eleven years, just before the end of slavery, Missy Tom suddenly gone one day from the estate. Carlos search and search but she was not found, neither heard of. Nobody had news if she was dead or locked away in a cellar somewhere for some wrong-doing.

Carlos had to go and work full-time, for his mother was not there to keep him. I heard he use to live very close to his mother and he never give up his hope of finding her alive.

Some years pass before Carlos find out that his mother and many other slaves was swapped for a few heads of cattle. Nega was yokemates with cattle and horses and the value was matched on them strength. It could be that this was one of the last times the bakkra make this kind of swap before slavery come to an end. But, me can tell you, it's about the only thing the bakkra didn't do when I was a boy.

Now slavery had come and gone in Antigua and we didn't have no apprenticeship[16] like them have to go through on the other islands, so Carlos — he was already living off the estate with some friends of his — went off on foot for a eighteen mile journey northwards to North Sound where his mother was suppose to be living. He find her there working at North Sound and decide to stay for the living condition was a trifle better than at Urlings where he use to be working. He had already passed forty years by then.

He had proper luck to find Missy Tom alive, for slaves back

16. Slaves in the other islands of the British West Indies had to serve an apprenticeship before full emancipation.

then hardly ever reach more than fifty-five years. He went to live common-law with Fancy at Freeman's Ville. This was the normal thing for the times, for it didn't have conflict with any religion[17] since there wasn't any church that catered to slaves and ex-slaves. It was there at Freeman's Ville that Fancy conceive of Henzel who, like me, got his name after the chief planter at Jonas. Henzel was therefore bound to work at Jonas.

My family get to be very close with the Weatherheads. Henzel get to be so famous for his strength that he get the nickname "All Man Giant". Everybody delight in his strength and the people and the bakkra have high regard for him. Even so, all that strength didn't save him tragedy. The yellow fever raging through the land took his mother and grandmother on the same day.

Because of his strength, the planters on Jonas had the habit of giving Henzel difficult tasks like rolling back the mills to clear the choke — to do by himself. He could also swing a sledge hammer easy as a machine.

As time pass, All Man Giant was given another job. He was the one to strap people to the whipping post. After some time Henzel refuse to do this and naturally this cause him to fall out of grace with the massa. Now that was the worse thing that could happen to him for it mean he was reduce to nothing. For a fact, death usually follow a fall out of grace.

Around 1889 or 1890 the bakkra at Jonas Estate decide to host the harvest feast. It was Henzel's job to make sure everything was in order and all the food and drinks ready. He also had to look after the horses and buggies of the guests.

You must remember that back then the harvest celebrations didn't have the religious feeling they have today. There would be a church service on the Sunday, but that service was just to herald the beginning of the estate owners' crop competition. A good harvest would mean hard work and not much pay for our people and the party was only for whites. After the planters had fill up them bellies and was most of the time too drunk and over-eat themselves to bother, we would nourish the leftovers.

17. See the introduction for the slave owners' attitudes towards slaves and religion.

The night before the harvest Henzel ate some bitter cassava and fell with the poison. Now he needed to be able to work so he took some molasses from the estate to cure the poison. He was so sick he couldn't knock a stroke that day.[18] It was his first and only time away from work. His companion went to see massa and try to tell him what had happen to her lover. The massa didn't want to hear anything about it, he drove her away. The next day Henzel force himself to return to Jonas to work. He attempt to get to Massa Arthur to explain what it was that happen to him.

He was greeted with annoyance. Massa Arthur was very upset because Henzel miss the great Harvest Sunday feast preparations. He sent a woman worker to drive Henzel off the estate, but Henzel insist he want to give explanation and there he remain. He was of the belief that he would be able to get his job back if he could get the massa to listen.

Instead, to Henzel's amazement, he was pounced upon and beaten by two white militiamen and they throw him off the estate.

The next day Henzel get summons to appear before the Parham Magistrate Court to face charges from what happen on Harvest Sunday. The charges read:

> Absent from duty, to the embarrassment of the Chief Planter, Arthur Smith and his distinguished guests.

and

> Stealing molasses from the said planter.

Henzel took his only chance and went back to Jonas to beg the planter to drop the charges. The law was that he would have to make good the damages, and get licks and jail if he was absent from work. Henzel also know the court was not going to be sympathetic, for them never was. When a planter would take a worker to court, the worker will get whatever the planter want for sentence.

When it come time for the trial Massa Arthur say that Henzel was unruly and disobedient. He say Henzel wouldn't obey and

18. Henzel was too ill to work.

that he refuse to strap the people for whipping. It seem to me the planters was just waiting for a reason to catch Henzel and the reason would not matter for they only want to get even with him. Henzel was not allowed to say a word in court. He get four months in jail, forty-eight strokes — twelve at the end of each month — and was banned from Jonas for six years.

Jail was hard work in those days. In fact, the other islands use to send their jail-men to Antigua to the work house, like we called it back then. As was common for the time, Henzel spent the first few weeks in jail locked to a seventy-five pound ball. He had to move about with it as best he could. He had more luck than some, though, for he was well-admired by the white jail guards for his strength and hard work. Henzel eventually get a pardon and get only twelve of the forty-eight mandatory strokes. He had luck in that because, back then, nothing sweet a white man more than drive licks under a black man's tail.

One time when Henzel was in jail he swallow down a sixpence piece to escape punishment. The money came from a visitor and he couldn't chance being seen with it, so he swallow the coin. That sixpence choke him for some time until he drink a dose of epsom salts to make it pass through his body.

Most of the time he was in the work house, he was sent to work on Delaps and Matthews estates. (Jail-men also use to work on the roads back then. Nearly all the roads was built by them men, but the planters also would get them to work free on estates, particularly in crop time.) After he get out he took a job at Matthews for the planters there admire[19] him while he was prisoner.

Henzel was not suppose to go through Jonas — so he have to use the long road from Clark's Hill to get to work. However, a bad wind never blow. Within a short space of time, his strength and hard work make him leader of one of the work gangs. He keep that job for many years.

Henzel die the same year my wife have our first child, Annie, in 1908. I still don't know for sure what happen to Henzel. The official talk was that he dead from yellow fever. No coroner's

19. The planters noticed Henzel's strength when he was a prisoner.

inquest for poor people in them days. When a nega man dead, he done.

People say that Henzel get poisoned. I think maybe Henzel's job breed grudge among his own people and maybe they just decide to wipe him out. One of our down fall is that some of the people get envious over one another for nothing. Life was so hard that one nega man hate to see another do well. Back then people would even have to carry them food on them, up and down in the field or factory because man scared somebody would put poison in they food. And people was too quick to blame yellow fever for the cause of certain deaths.

Henzel left one son call Samuel. He went to Panama and never come back.

Up to this day I wonder what the truth is. Was it the refusal of Henzel to help the planters beat the people that result in revenge on him? Was there other things I didn't know about? Henzel was the only black man at Matthews, maybe in Antigua, that could ask the massa to grant pardon to a person and get it. When we start the union I was always thinking of Henzel. I always wish that he was around.

Work was hell. Back in them days, sugar cane was tied in bundles before they was packed into the carts and taken to the mills. That was the system they use, to keep the canes from falling out on the way to the mills and also to keep canes from remaining in the fields. Workers would get paid by the weight of the canes. Your pay would be short if canes was found on the road or left back in the fields. The animals that would pull the carts was not always too easy to control and the roads was rough. And you have to take special care when you pack the cane into the cart to make sure that it was in there as tight as possible.

It was the job of the cutters to get their own tiers to tie up the bundles. These tiers was paid from the wages of the cutters that hire them. Sometimes women worked as the tiers for their husbands to keep all the money in the family. It was also usual for the tiers to help the cutters to cut the canes. All this was done to make as much money as possible and keep the money in the family.

Missy Count Paul was a tier at Jonas Estate. It was close to Easter in the year 1890. What happen to Missy Count Paul was one of the reasons why my mother did not want me to work at Jonas and why I well-remember that year.

Count didn't come back to work after lunch one day. Sometime in the afternoon, Massa Ben, one of the planters in charge of the reaping, saw her lying in the shade near the canefield that was being reaped at the time. He didn't know who she was. Any worker that was found lying in the shade, particularly at reaping time, was inviting serious trouble. The punishment could be licks, jail, heavy fines, or the planter could throw you out if you would have lodging on the estate.

Massa Ben, on reaching close, saw that the person was Missy Count Paul. She appear to be sleeping. He decide to gallop the horse and frighten her. He went some distance away and then gallop the horse at full speed. He guide it up to the lady. The sound of the horse did not stir her and the horse run over her. Missy Count Paul did not shake one bit.

A little time pass when Missy Count Paul's boy, Matthew, come upon his mother in the canefield. She look all mash up. Matthew could not stir her. He goes and gets the village doctor[20] and then goes to find Massa Ben so he can get a note for the doctor to attend to her. When Matthew find Massa Ben he explain in full the condition of his mother. Matthew get the note from Massa Ben and he take the note speedily to Dr. Williams at Vernon's Estate. Now Matthew didn't know what was in the note, but he believe it explain the problem and that the doctor would come to Freeman's Ville to attend to his mother, for there was no way to carry somebody to the doctor.

When the doctor read the note he say, "Bury the woman". Poor young Matthew was struck dumb. He couldn't believe him ears. Back then, remember, nega never take courage to speak up to the massa. Matthew knew his mother wasn't dead when he went for the doctor, but still he could not speak to lord and massa Dr. Williams. He went away with the paper the doctor gave him.

20. Village women who were healers. Chapter 3 discusses their role and the treatments they devised.

Now in them days the people was plenty obedient and Matthew was just like everybody else. He never give any thought to opening that letter. Now me, I figure a man with any sense would open up that letter, but fooly Matthew did not. No, he went and give the letter to Ben. The massa then told him to go collect the coffin that same day. Matthew went back to Freeman's Ville and explain what happen to the family. Well Missy Count Paul still not dead, so the family refuse to go and collect the coffin. The village doctor keep on trying to wake her.

The next day two horse guards that come and visit the sick ask for the family of Missy Count Paul. This was Matthew. One of the horse guards tell Matthew and the others that was present at the time that Missy was a witch and fell in a chance[21] at mid-day so her spirit would not be able to find the body again. Therefore, he say, she ought to be buried. The family and the villagers very well knew that Missy was not dead, but them have to make up their minds to lose her. Massa say bury and she must be bury. Up to the time she was in place in the coffin her followers was still listening to hear if she would cry out. Them two horse guards stay until the coffin was all seal up.

We know nothing about rights in them days. Massa was the only rightful person. I was just a little boy, but sensible enough to know what was going on. What I know is that the English bakkra was mortally afraid of witchcraft.[22] You get caught doing witchcraft and you would never miss the jail-house and the cat-o-nine. You would be lucky to get out alive and if you do, you would be bruise all over.

Back then many people didn't know the difference when a person was in a deep sleep or actually dead. It is true to say this even of doctors themselves because some people escape being put in the ground alive even after they was in the coffin. Douglas Myers of Parry and Diamond Estate was pronounce dead. Them even have the wake. Douglas was placed in his coffin and we was singing funeral hymns. The hymn reader was there showing off, as was the custom, and Douglas parents was just waiting on the hour to put the lid on him when he suddenly start to turn and

21. Trance.
22. For information of the law prohibiting the practice of obeah, see Appendix B.

twist. The people that first saw the hands and then his head move sure scamper out of the house quick. Finally Douglas get up out of his coffin.

The case of Missy Count Paul was different. She perish from deliberate murder. Her death be part and parcel of what happen to our people in Antigua for many years, even years after slavery was suppose to come to an end. Tongue can't tell of the many wickedness that use to happen to us — for the bakkra didn't think that slavery was over.

I live there at Jonas Estate for a little over ten years. My mother did everything she could to get us off the estate and she share in that wish with many others. My mother look at estate after estate, but all was the same. The cry at Marrow was the same cry at Briggin — horrible. She therefore decide not another estate for her.

3

Village Life:
It Wasn't Just the Doctoring We Have To Do for Ourself

One of the happiest moments in the life of my family took place in 1888. In that year we built our own house at Freeman's Ville, the second village put up after freedom come.

My grandmother told me that at first people called the village Franchie Bell, but the people that live there changed the name because they were always rebellious. (She also used to talk about Liberta village, the first village that the nega people set up after freedom in 1834, and how that village got its name from the word liberty. The people pick up the word from the American way of talking about freedom.)

When we start to build our house a Methodist minister, one Rev. James, helped my father to get some second-hand materials from Jonas Estate. The materials, together with some local wood, was put together to construct the house.

At last we were under our own roof and enjoying, for the first time, family privacy. Estate life was behind our back at last.

My parents set about the tasks of settling down and bringing us up the best way possible. The open vice that my mother fear so much on the estates was not displayed in the village. The village was indeed a quiet place.

Before the villages begin to grow, there was two groups of negas in Antigua, the nega-house man and the town man. The villages shape another group, the country man. The village man generally was feeling that he was better than the estate man and the town man was feeling he was better than everybody.

Times change slowly, but village life continue to develop. We use to go to the Methodist church school at Freeman's Ville. There was no writing books in them days. We learnt to write on slates with a chalk-like stone we called aboo. And when it was possible my mother would send us to church on Sundays. The village was of no size to speak of. There were the Methodist church and some three or four houses that belong to the church, but the village itself was just some twelve houses. That village had less houses in it when I was a boy than shortly after the time of the Emancipation. People couldn't afford to build a house then.

Building houses in the village were slow back in them days. It was real hard to get a house. You have to have proper luck to be able to get into village life. I remember that some fourteen months happen to pass after our house was built before another family was able to settle in at Freeman's Ville.

You have to keep in mind that in them days there was nobody to speak up for us. Nobody. It seem to me that there was not one single person that have the right to talk up or represent anybody. No, we lived and worked back then as massa say.

There was widespread hunger, there were starvation. I am not lying: there was not a single one of us that did not suffer terrible hunger. Now we wanted to work the land that was not in use so we would not have to bear that hunger. There was mass unemployment and the wages for the ones that was lucky enough to have a job was just a pittance.

People was so poor they didn't like to go to work when it was raining because you would only have one set of clothes. If your clothes get wet, they would have to dry on you or you could take them off and stay naked. Nowadays we have lots of clothes, but people still don't like to go and work when it rain.

We were bound and determined to work the land. Back then, the planters was very well aware that no race work harder than we. If we could work the land, then in process of time we would become self-sufficient or we would be in control of things.

But the bakkra knew very well that was the main artery to independence for we. They was also well aware that if we have land we will have no need to work cheap for them. You see, if we have our own land, this will be the biggest threat to the British Empire, so all the land was massa's own; nega man own nothing. From what I know, the British attitude to any and all of the ex-slaves anywhere was exactly the same as far as the land goes. Them never want us to work the land. All the feast and fuss them behave with amount to one thing; them afraid black people come to boss them.

But as time pass, them have to let us work the land. For sure, though, the Englishmen was very careful how they go about that. Whenever we get permission to farm, the bakkra remain the full owners of the produce. Not less than half of the area was to be planted in sugar cane. We could cultivate, plant and care the field, but the planters keep the right to decide when would the reaping take place. Them also have the right to say if the persons that worked in the fields should get any of the produce.

If massa felt that the persons deserve a portion of the produce, well no doubt they would get that portion. If his decision happen to be to the contrary, then it would be just hard luck for them. Them work for nothing and that's it. The disgraceful thing was, we couldn't say a word. Not a blessed word. So you can imagine, if you had the privilege to work the land you would sure try and stay well within the good graces of massa.

As time pass, things gradually change. More planters continue to go back to England and, step by step, a larger portion of land became available. There was room for us to build up the villages.

But although we would have some land, the lack of building materials and money seriously hinder us. You see, before going back to England, most of the bakkra would go and tear down some of the old estate houses that belong to them. They would sell the materials second-hand to the people and them materials would sure be in great demand. Now that stuff was far from being enough to provide for the great need of the people that wish to leave the estates, so there was always a serious rush by the people to get the torn down materials. Sometimes the planters would stop the public sale and sell privately to the chosen ones. People that did not have the fortunate position to buy the second-hand wood, but were determined to move away from the estates, would build the houses from wood from the caps[1] and from trash and mud. We call them wattle and daub houses. For many years most of the houses on the island was comprise of wattle and daub.

Even when you got your house built, you still have to reckon with natural ills: hurricanes, earthquakes and drought. The wattle and daub houses and most of the ones built by second-hand materials could hardly stand up to hurricanes or the gale force winds. Winds with far less force have severely damaged the trash houses from time to time. This was particularly the case in 1899 when Antigua was hit by gale force winds. Freeman's Ville at that time was comprise of some twenty houses and more than half that number was completely destroyed.

The people of Freeman's Ville was allow to live in the cellar of the Methodist Church in times of hurricanes. If your house was destroyed, you was allowed to stay in the cellar until you could find other means of shelter. After the hurricane of 1899, the people of Freeman's Ville did not rebuild the houses at the original spot. They were built instead some half a mile eastward. In process of time, all the people move from the original spot of Freeman's Ville and settled in at the new site. We use the opportunity to build the houses on land that was left lie by the planters.

You know, it was always difficult for me to decide which of the two ills was the worse, drought or hurricane, or which one cause more suffering on the people.

I think severe drought were more prevalent than hurricanes or gale force winds. Hurricanes would smash up our homes and we would have to start life all over again. But it's still very difficult to say which of them cause more agony back then. The way it was, you see, the planters usually would use the drought as an

1. Areas covered with trees and bush.

excuse to cut the wages — and the pay was already very low — and people trying to get a job would find it rough because the planters was deliberately refusing to hire people.

Food was always hard to come by, but this situation would be severely worsen by the drought so hunger and starvation was more common then. Many of our people serve time in the jail house or got licks for using the bakkra's food or water. Even during the dry weather we could not use the pond water without permission. Life was indeed sheer misery.

Some time close to the end of the century, Joe Martin, a cousin of mine from Freeman's Ville, was charge for stealing a bucket of water from Old Pond at North Sound Estate. That same year, we face a severe drought and water for the village was plenty scarce. Now Joe went to the North Sound head planter to make up the case. Joe knew that he could not escape prison if the case be heard by the magistrate and also there was still the possibility for him to get the order for licks in prison. He therefore decide to be whipped by the planter at North Sound. Well, them maltreat Joe. He nearly dead and he did not catch himself for a long time. Joe lived to a ripe old age but didn't get rid of the scars that he receive from them blows.

The food situation did not get better. The food sent from England was not for us but for the planters and them families. The leftovers was sold to people, but most of the times that food were unfit for human consumption. The rice, the flour and cornmeal was generally full of worms. We would use a sifter to separate the worms but the smell of the goods was usually unpleasant.

Despite the bad quality of the goods in the shops, the lines was long and the noise and quarrel to get serve was terrible. Some of the times fights broke out amongst people that force themselves into the line. The goods we readily used to eat back then are what people use to feed pigs with today. We ate them and survived. It would also be fair to say that we were surviving mainly from the crumbs that fell from the massa's table. Many a hungry soul await those crumbs.

Somehow we try and manage. The relish usually used were saltfish, shad and other pickled meat, and tango — when we could get it. Cassie, paw-paw, spinach, pusley, and other vegetables was also added together with the shad, fish or meat, as the case may be. Corn was also eaten very often. We would roast it, boil it or make it into hashum by roasting and grinding it with sugar. Then we would eat the hashum for a main meal, usually lunch. There's not many young people today know that food, or maybe people don't eat it anymore.

Back then nearly every house use to have a mortar and pestle and that tool we would use to make hashum, coffee, and them things.

Ground provision such as potatoes, yams, cassavas and pumpkins — when the pumpkins was available — was use in many different ways. Potatoes at most times was boiled or roasted and eaten with shad and saltfish. At other times, we would take it and make potato soup or pudding. Maybe you will not believe this, but one piece of shad use to serve the family for a week. We dipped the fungi on the shad, but sometimes things were of such that we could not eat it off at once.

Cassava are of two kinds, the bitter and the sweet. The sweet cassava is boiled and eaten with any kind of relish. The bitter cassava is poisonous if you boil and eat it. It will cause you severe pain in the stomach and vomiting. That kind of cassava have to be grated, and the liquid along with certain amount of starch, taken off. Then you dry out the flour and make it into bread or bamboola. The starch was used in the washing of clothes. People clothes sure use to be stiff on them.

The coconut was one of the most important fruits in them days. It was for making coconut tarts, sugar cakes, coconut dumplings, coconut syrup and other tasty foods. With our homemade coconut oil we use to fry up dumplings and meat. It was also for greasing the hair and skin. That oil was also good for cruffie skins, stiff joints and chest colds.

Now, Antigua is not blessed with wild life, so that kind of meat usually was scarce. The better off villagers will have them pig and will keep that pig until Christmas. But it was tango or no meat at all for long periods. There were not many fishermen at that time, and the few that were there could not explore the sea to the full. That was because there was a lack of proper boats and nets, so you couldn't get much sea food to speak of. Sometimes we would set out crab boxes and large crowds of young men usually go searching for crabs and cockles. Fungi with crab was a kind of national dish for us. Mind you, many times it was crab alone on the table. It's funny, but people couldn't drink water after eating crab, for the taste of the water was bitter like gall. What the people drink instead was sugar water — we call bebish.

When we start to work land, we planted ginger and that drink was tasty indeed. Sorrel drink came once a year — the Christmas drink. We also have the custom to make drinks from Annie seed and some people would use that plant also to make wine. We would plant our pepper and make our vinegar from the cane juice. For many years the pepper vinegar was locally made.

There are also some trees that I can never forget. Them help and make life in those days. The mange dagger was use to make the fences for the houses. If you find where the dagger is growing, well that is a sign that people use to live in the area. We call its stalk "dagger long" and the tree die after it appear. When the dagger was dry the fishermen used to use it to make small boats. The mangeneel tree was use to frame the house. It is a very poisonous tree and no moth can eat the wood. When the mangeneel get on the skin it is like acid, the juice blister and burn the skin. We were always very careful when we went to cut it. The cedar tree was to frame the house. Cedar is a very good wood, it's strong and will last you for a long time. The planters, too, used to use it to make knares for cart wheels. Then there was the bamboo and the tamarind tree that were use to make fish pots and the bread basket, a very important thing. I say bread, but the bakkra would say dung baskets. That basket was the thing we have for drop out the dung at the sugar cane roots. The bark of the turkey feed or claman cherry tree was use to make rope. And nobody in Antigua can ever forget the old calabash tree. That calabash tree was also a big help. We use the old calabash to make food and water containers.

We make nearly everything we used. Our coffee was from jumbie beads, wild tamarinds and warri seeds. The seeds were all roast and grounded together. People don't worry with that coffee today, but it was the best coffee. And there was also all kinds of plants we use to make tea — fever grass, cassie balsam, lime bush, noyo-seige, cattle tongue, sour sop and mother sydril. Trible grape, old man beard, French thyme, sweet mint, baricada bush, porter bush, jugger man bush, man-pan tree, long grass, blackberry, polly pojer and St. John bush. The Christmas bush was use to give taste to cocoa, tea and pap, and so too were orange and lemon skins.

Nearly every grown adult have them pipe to smoke, made from bamboo stalks. The home-grown tobacco leaves was left to dry out and smoked in place of the good tobacco because, in them days, hardly any money was there to buy the imported kind. That tobacco tree was precious to us. Snuff too was a comforter for our people when the goings get rough and there wasn't enough to eat. Nearly every worker was taking snuff in my time.

Now lighting that tobacco — or a piece of wood, for that matter — was not like today. Matches were scarce and could not be had for long periods. What we did was to use the home-made tinder box to light the fire in place of matches. Tinder boxes was made up of a piece of cotton stuffed tightly inside of a piece of cattle horn. You take the cotton and stuff it into the horn to keep all the cotton from catching ablaze at once. Then you take a file and rub it against a piece of flinstone to make the spark that lights the cotton. If you don't have a file, two pieces of flinstone will do fine. I'd like to give credit to the tinder box specialist of Antigua, a man by the name of Buxy Dean of Freeman's Ville. We used to make rhyme on him like this:

Oh, Missa Dean, go light de tinder box,
Me na ha no match, me na need no match
Missa Dean got to mek de tinder box.

Knives, forks and spoons was very hard to come by so we make them too. Forks and spoons was out of wood. The good calabash tree also provide us some very handy things for the kitchen and the hard-working people of Sea View Farm was providing the pottery to complete the necessary conveniences of the home. In them days, we didn't know what was called ice. Instead we have the long jar to keep the water cool. The people of Sea View Farm also made the long jar.

You might be surprised to know this, but we didn't get pipe-borne water in the villages for many, many years. You couldn't collect water from a thatch-roof house and there was no large containers for storing drinking water back then. Ponds was made by the villagers to provide them with water. The catchment made to provide the people of Freeman's Ville with water was named after the man that select the spot, a man by the name of Punchey. Up to today the area is still known as Punchey. Even today when the rain comes that catchment still will hold little water. Now life has changed considerably since then and few people today even know how that spot got its name.

As time change everything, the planters begin to let their workers use the estate pond water from time to time. But this did not put an end to the problem of getting water. The pond water was very unclean because plenty crapaud[2] was living in them pond. And them crapaud use to make wash tun a noise a night-time.[3] They use to ball for joy. You see, animal too usually pass their urine and waste while drinking water. Now that kind of water was always dangerous for health. We gladly drink that water, though, nothing else min dey.[4] It's like this: a crapaud and animal waste water, man use it and survive.

Now the bakkra was always afraid of diseases. Still and all, they took quite a long time before they did anything to clean up the place. While our people was struggling to make the new and independent village life, many of them dead. Typhoid fever, malaria, yellow fever, ulcer, T.B., hunger, tetanus, and other deadly diseases was killing a lot of our people. It was common for a family to have more than one person die in a short time. And quite a few planter was dying too. Massa Hinds of North Sound had two sons that die from typhoid fever. The Goodwins at Collins also lost a sister from yellow fever.

Disease was indeed a problem. Now, very few trained doctors was around and they were not interested to attend to poor black people, so we just have to make up our minds to live without them and use our own means to make life more easy. For

2. Frogs.
3. The sound of frogs croaking was very loud at night.
4. They had no choice but to drink the water.

example, there was always a local village doctor. Now whether it was by accident or by design, I don't know, but the local village doctor was always a woman. I can't remember even one man that know very much local remedy. These women doctors knew the local remedy for all kinds of things, the best bush for the particular sickness. Some people was cured, others wasn't. The important thing was them women sure try. Them did their best to help.

The bush syrup, for colds and so on, was made up of mangy dagger, eucalyptus, sage and cattle tongue leaves along with bark mixed up with sugar. Sissle, bamboo bush and French thyme was also capital for colds. To clean the blood you would take and boil white head broom and law lavington bush together with bitter mint and inflammation bush. The sixty-six bush was also a good blood cleaner. And tizan bush tea and tanbrana root water were use by men to keep them cross.[5] We indeed use to love and cherish them bush.

There was also the blood pressure bush and the love bush that the blessed bush doctor usually give you for kidney and liver sickness. And the heart bush was capital for heart problems. The human milk was the remedy for sore eyes.

The women also knew to boil up the root of the powerful doctor dull-dull bush for the painful monthly things. And later it was found that maiden blush bush was good for blood pressure and headaches and that brackish jelly water will serve for rheumatism and arthritis. The friendly and helpful village doctor also have what was the best cure for insect bites and stings — rub the spot with three different kinds of bush — and that too was capital. The sweetheart and inflammation bushes was the remedy use for the stoppage of water, for men use to suffer regularly from the various kinds of venereal diseases. That inflammation bush was well-known to all the men. So too women use vervine tea to clean them when pregnant and sage tea was for baby gripe. But the amazing cure to stop nagging belly gripe was to put the person across the doorway to lie down, put your foot in the belly and quarrell. The belly gripe would then stop.

5. Used to ensure male potency.

Roast potatoes and salt butter was the remedy for mumps. The worm grass was for worms and you would use turpentine for boils and heat. Senna and epsom salts was the remedy for almost everything. For a fact, epsom salts was over-used and sometimes people dead from it. Soap and sugar was for poultice and castor leaf bush was to cool down fever and blood pressure. Aloes mixed with gin was the cure for sugar.[6]

The leaves of the large pain killer tree at North Sound Estate was to cure pain. Whoever pick the leaves must pay the tree, either with a coin or a ten-penny nail. People say that if you did not pay the tree, the leaves would be of no effect and the pain would not get better. Back then the people truly believe in that story and pay the tree at all times. The nails and coins are still there for all to see.

The best village doctor also have the knowledge to refit dislocated ribs back into the right place. The bakkra doctors wasn't competent in this. Them never could do that job better than the women that serve as village doctors. Them women do everything to lessen the sufferings of our poor people. "There is a tree to cure every sickness and a tree to suit every purpose" — that was their belief. God bless them.

Our people also was suffering from toothache. It was the normal thing for the face to be twist out of shape because of bad teeth. False teeth was not around back then. The way things was, we hardly even hear of dentists. We used to use charcoal and peas bush to clean the teeth. I was lucky. I never had bad teeth in my young days. The first time I ever go and see a dentist, I was close to eighty years old.

It wasn't just the doctoring that we have to do for ourself. In those days, except for the moon and stars, there was no lights. Quite early in the evening the kerosene lamps would be put out for fear of fire. We would make our lamps called dunkey pumps. At night that village was dead for sure and the land was almost covered up by sugar cane and sea island cotton. Now most people was afraid of the dark nights and when the moon was up, we use to pray for it to stay on forever. Then, as that could not be, the honest prayer was for its speedy return.

6. Diabetes.

And for many years nobody had idea of what a clock was like. It was the moon or stars to judge the time at nights or early mornings and we have to judge the daylight hour by a stick or the length of our shadow. But you know, them two planets fool us many times.

I remember that one of the big differences between life on the estates and village life was that we could play our own music as hard as we want — something that was strictly forbidden on the estates. (But even with this difference, you better have manners towards the older folks. Parents used to beat them picknee for the slightest thing. You could not whistle in front of an older person because that was rude. Even the older children used to beat up on the little ones. I believe this come down from slavery times and that our folks just carry it on. Nowadays people just love them picknee and treat them like king and queen.) Anyway, we would just make whatever noise we like and beat the African rhythm whenever we want. Most of the times we made music with pieces of iron or tin pans and sometimes with the flamboyant shack shack. Another difference was that the kooka bendal was far from the houses.

We built tents and held singing meetings, concerts and dances. The tents was also to keep night schools. If you did not get the opportunity to go to school, and had an interest to learn something, you would flock to the tents because, you see, after village life start to develop our people was desperate to learn how to read.

Now some of the finest speeches and keenest speaking competitions would take place at the singing meetings. There was also a singing competition at those meetings. The speakers usually would speak on topics from the Bible mixed with verses of famous poems or hymns. Even people that couldn't read would get up and speak at singing meetings. The songsters would sing from the sacred songs and spiritual hymn books. The best singers and speakers would get prizes. You would have to get dressed up proper, too. You wasn't allowed to speak at them singing meetings if you did not wear a jacket. Now in them days, we did not have such comfort, so we use to borrow jacket from some of the bakkra and them, and that jacket sometimes have to be used by all the speakers. The ladies' dresses back then was well passed the knee, the neck was pinned or buttoned up and the sleeves well passed the arm. Women also wear jumbie beads and warry beads around the neck to help them beautify themselves. The gals them look good.

But, life was not all work, or making things to use or getting bush or singing in the tents. During Lent nearly every man was spinning tops and we would fly the kites in the hot months when the turkey berries was ripe. Sometimes you could be at Freeman's Ville and hear them kites humming over at Sea View Farm. We would also play cashew and when cashew time was out, marble time would come in.

There were also times of grief. In our grief too, it was the practice to give our dead meaningful farewell by having "wakes". Anybody could give out hymns at the "wakes", but that person would then have to read the hymn loud, line by line, while the rest of the people would sing. The reader of the hymn dare not make mistake or that person would be chided very severely. Those "wakes" was reading practice for us. There would be food too. Strong coffee and biscuits — when available — would be eaten to keep our eyes open until morning broad.

Mark you, there was no undertakers back then. Everybody have to bury them dead and the dead have to stay in the house until the next day. Maybe that was the main reason for "wakes".

A bunch of grass would be placed on the belly of the dead to keep it from rising. People had to bear the dead from their homes to the church. All the houses would be closed down where the funeral procession was passing. In similar manner, women use to turn their dresses over their head when walking at nights and men use to turn their shirts on the wrong side. The bearers of the coffin have to carry six gravel stones to keep the dead from putting too much weight on them.

If there would be a young picknee living in the house, the parents would usually have a ritual. Two people would stand on each side of the dead and the child would then be toss over the dead three times to keep the jumbie[7] from coming back to interfere with the picknee.

7. Ghost or spirit.

The people in my days was superstitious to the proper. On the first day of each month, before my old people got out of bed, they use to shout "Rabbit, Rabbit, Rabbit!" to bring them some kind of good luck — at least for the remainder of the month. And that was the way almost all the people was behaving back then. People use to be mortally afraid of black cats. Whenever one would run across the road, or whenever people met up with them, they would get very disturbed, for the were of the belief that was bad luck for sure.

Children were warned against counting stars, for if they did, the belief was that not less than three people from the village will die in a short time. It was also a serious matter to turn back; back then people seldom turn back for anything. It would have to be something that was of extreme importance to get a person to turn back and if you was forced to turn back, you must then spin around three times in the road to prevent the sure bad luck that was destined to meet you.

You would never find a single woman sitting on a table. She was also certain to get out of the way if somebody was sweeping for the broom must not touch her feet. The belief was that if any of these things happen, she would never get a husband. And back then, it was also the case that a pregnant woman would never be found around a butcher's stall when an animal was being killed or the picknee would be born with some defects. If the animal was a goat, the babe would have the face of a goat. She must also not feel sorry for anything for that would also affect the babe.

In the old days, anybody that was throwing away a piece of bread first must soak that bread in water. If that wasn't done, bad luck would follow the person for a long time. So too, it was said that if a person throw away salt that person must wet the place, or throw one of the grains behind without looking back, or else bad luck was sure to befall that person.

And you know, I think that even up to now some people are still of the belief that the first person you see in the morning will determine the kind of day you will have. You see, it was the belief that if you see a lazy man first thing in the morning, then you will feel lazy throughout the day. The opposite will be the case if the first person you see is jolly and hardworking. But it was a happy thing when a cock crew more than once in front the door for a good visitor was bound to show up.

If a window be converted into a door, then the head of the house must kill a cock as a sacrifice, or somebody in that house was sure to die. Also, if a hen crows it is a bad sign and the owner of that hen must destroy it.

It was also the belief that if a huckster[8] leave home without selling something, that huckster may not have a good selling day. She would have the same fate if an enemy happen to be the first to buy from her in the morning.

Whenever a dog would hound[9] at night it was definite that somebody's spirit was walking. In similar manner people would say that if somebody whistle in the night, that person was calling a spirit.

Every village would have its obeah man or woman. I remember there was the coffee[10] woman that people use to check out to know what was going on or what would happen in the future. It was not a joke. The people believed in the superstition and the rituals.

Back then times were hard. And man do anything to survive. The women not only find remedy for the sick but was brave. My grandmother use to talk of a woman call Missy Williams, the first woman to leave Pinchin Estate after slavery end. She went to live in the "jar", a rock people use to go in or under during bad weather. The massas at Pinchin Estate send some people to break up the rock. In other words to destroy Missy Williams' dwelling place. But she fight the people off. Missy Williams continued to live in that area for some time after this incident. In my younger days that area was called Jausha Long Hall. My grandmother also use to talk of a slave woman call Lav Lav: she learn the language quick and was caught teaching the English to other slaves, a thing that was not allowed. She was severly beaten and then sold to another estate owner. My grandmother talk of

8. Vendor in the open-air market.
9. Howl.
10. Fortune teller.

two women, Bessy and Mary or Manda who play a major role to save the Methodist religion after the founder dead. You see, in those days women do everything. They even make pots from clay, a thing men hardly take interest in.

4
The Powerful: Massa Was King and King Do No Wrong

The great happiness over our new settlement was not to last for too long. In 1890 trouble show its face. A fire completely destroyed the house. I cannot tell you the sorrow that rip the family, but never will I forget that day. It was my first real sad moment, maybe the saddest in my life. My mother bawl till she nearly drop.

Because of the fire my family made two important decisions. The first was that we would never go back to living on a plantation; the second was that whatever happen, the family must not be broke up — that none of us would go to live somewhere else.

For a time the Methodist Church let us live in the cellar of one of the houses next to the village. During the stay at the Methodist house we build a tent-like house out of wattle and thrash[1] near the spot of the burnt-out one. That house have no floor, but it was fairly comfortable — except when it rain.

1. Wood, mud and trash construction; usually the door was the only source of light in this type of house.

We had the determination to build our home again, but if we want to do that quickly, we would have to make a lot of sacrifice. I felt it was my bounden duty, being one of the oldest, to quit school and go to work to help make sure we wouldn't have to go back to living on the estates. It seem to me that the place to go and look for a job was at Jonas Estate. My father was working there and he was one of the nega people that have a reasonable good relationship with the planters on that estate. We also use to live at Jonas for some time when I was small and it was Jonas we left from to settle at Freeman's Ville. It surprised me, but both my mother and father have strong objection to me going to work at Jonas. They was mortally afraid that I would get to be a victim at Jonas, for there was brutal things happening on that estate nearly every day.

After some talk on the matter my mother decide that I must go to North Sound Estate and try it there. I was ready to do anything to help out the family, so I went to North Sound and join the small gang there. I was thirteen years old. The first day I work, I was surprised to find out that a lot of picknee in the gang was younger than me.

One of the first things I learnt at North Sound was that we could not talk to each other at work. As soon as you reach the estate's works[2] all talk must stop. In fact, gathering together was strictly not allowed. If massa would see us talking, we have to say what the talk was about. (One of the worst things about that, though, was that certain black people seem to always take great pleasure to lie on their own kind to massa and quite a lot of innocent people would get punish because of that. Sometimes, though, the news carriers suffer worse than the people them carry the news on.)

My first job was to drop out dung at sugar cane roots. I can't remember what the pay was — for the first three years I work, it was my mother that would collect the money. As a rule, the planters usually didn't pay money to picknee. The few time I happen to collect the pay, I couldn't open up the cloth it was tied up in. Anyway, I felt it was my mother's duty to collect the pay, so I wasn't too interested in that.

2. The ground of the estate.

We always was of the belief that where there's a will there's a way, so two years or so after the fire we rebuilt the house on the same spot. Once again we were so happy for that house. Like my mother say, no more horrors on the estate. She sure mean that, too. But my mother didn't know that the times at North Sound was going to be more perilous.

I was lucky to escape the brutality there at North Sound. I worked hard and I also would have a lot of manners. People say that manners and good behaviour carry you through the world and it surely carry me safely up to this day. I never go and interfere with anybody and I was obedient: nobody have to tell me to do something more than once. But the goings was rough, rough against our own people.

Back then there were laws to keep people from doing cruel things to animals, but there was no laws to protect us from cruelty. Now I'm not a lawyer, but what I know is that I've seen a lot of our people get sent to the jail-house, get whipped and suffer other things if they happen to mark an animal with a whip, but I have never seen nor hear of a white man being punish for anything he do to one of us. Massa was king and king do no wrong.

The first murder I witness at North Sound was when Harty Bab get killed. Back then the planters use to call the names of the workers each day before the start of work. Our money would be stopped or the bakkra could take us to the magistrate if we was not present to answer to our names. When our names was called we have to answer, "Yes, Massa." Now, the names was not called at any set time, like 6:00 a.m. or 7:00 a.m. No, massa would just call the names in his own sweet time and we just have to make sure we were there to answer. Sometimes we would be feeling we were early, but then we were late. Other times we'd be thinking we late and then we early.

One morning after the roll call, we have to wait for orders from the planter in charge of the gang. While we were there waiting, Massa Hinds youngest boy, Ralph, starts to imitate his father and goes calling our names. Everybody answer like usual, until he gets to Harty Bab. At least she didn't answer, "Yes, Massa." Now Massa Hinds was close by, and he tell her that she was marked absent for not answering. He say she disrespect his son and she was not going to get pay for that day. Then he further accuse her of grumbling bad words at him. In the end he so annoyed he decide to lash her with a cart whip. When he try this, she resist him, but that didn't last for too long for she was over-powered and he beat her mercilessly. Then he forced her into the estate cellar where he leave her locked up for some days.

When he give the order to release her, she was dead. Rats had bitten off her lips and nose.

Remember that whatever we have in mind to say to massa about this, we have to keep it to ourselves. If anybody want to cry for Harty, it best be in quiet or away from the estate. Only women and the small gang workers was seen around the estate that day, for when the news break that Harty Bab dead and have no lips or nose on her face, all the men scamper. (I didn't see any sense in that because the massa was a local constable and could give orders in the name of the Queen to anybody.) They was afraid that the massas would order them in the name of the Queen to take the body out of the cellar.

I was at that cellar and saw the body. I'll never forget that day. I was fifteen years old and still in the small gang, doing a man's job for a boy's pay.

Later that same morning, a white man came on the estate, he look on the body, say few words to massa, and then left. Harty's people went for the body and the estate provide them with the coffin. They took her away in a horse and cart for burying. Harty's body couldn't be kept till the next day so we didn't have a wake for her, just a singing funeral.

Later in the week, I hear a rumour that the white man that come and look at the body was the magistrate and that he say Harty dead from "misadventure". When I get to be much older I learnt the meaning of that word — that's the word that was always used to say what was the cause of that kind of death.

That was the end of Harty. Nobody give notice to the brutal murder done by Massa Hinds, planter and local constable of North Sound Estate.

It seem them estate cellars was even specially built to torture slaves. They was dark and when the doors was closed you couldn't see nothing. Scarcely any air could pass through and they was filled with vicious rats and other harmful creatures. People that was locked up in the dungeon even for a day and escape death was lucky. Only the planters could say should the two air holes be open or not. If they was closed tight, the person couldn't last for long.

Back then, the bakkra use to keep a lot of cattle and horses. They used to use them to supply milk and meat and these things was very important to the upkeep of the planters. You know, cattle and sugar was the kings and queens of the Empire. Horses was also pulling the sugar canes, but the main use was to carry massa and friends. They was like the buses and cars of today.

The groom was the worker that have the job to take care of the horses. He would get a room on the estate and he usually would be thinking he better than the other workers on the estate. The groom was very close to massa and he would do everything to keep in his good graces, so he was the errand boy and the news carrier too. Most of us didn't trust the groom for we believe he was a stooge.

A groom that work at North Sound Estate for a number of years during my time was one Meryl Jacobs of Potters Village. Suddenly, it happen that the estate's calves start to be let loose at nights from time to time and then there was no milk the next morning. This gave the planters the suspicion that one of the workers was letting the calves loose so they decide to do something to catch the smady.[3]

They begin to quietly lie wait at night a little way from the animals and lo and behold, one night they come upon Meryl the groom with a bag wrapped around him, milking one of them cows. They grab him, tie both hands together, then tie him to the end of the cattle chain. Now we believe them beat he before them tie him to the chain. The cattle drag Meryl all over the place till morning. When we go to work in the morning, the bakkra call all the workers to look at Meryl at the end of the cattle chain with his tongue out of his mouth stiff dead.

The planters say he was the scamp. The workers say it was a good thing he got his hands caught in that chain for if not, massa

3. Somebody.

would blame them. The estate provide coffin for Meryl. His people took the body away and that was the end of him. The planters just laugh and say look what happen if you steal. Nobody investigate. In fact, nobody die — Meryl was just a bird or a thing.

Ever so often when we was working we would jump when the whip crack behind us. Workers was mortally afraid of that whip and if you got hit, you just have to take it to the Lord in prayer. Every man, woman and child 'fraid the whip. This make people try and speed up the work, and a lot of workers, particularly cane cutters, use to get hurt when they try and make more speed than they could control.

I remember the time we was building the road between Old Pond and North Sound works and we have to pull the cart full up with stone from about a mile away. Massa Barnette come and start to crack the whip behind us. He hit a man by the name of Quallis in the eye. Quallis eventually lose that eye. Some months pass and one day the chief planter, Massa Hinds go and crack the whip behind a gang of cane cutters. Now Papa Joe, a man from North Sound, tell old Hinds that his eye won't go for nothing. Papa Joe was ordered off the estate and later on that day he was arrested by two horse guards for "intent to do grievous bodily harm" to the massa. They beat him on the head and knees. Pape Joe live on that estate all his life, but that was that.

People wanted to put a small house together for Papa Joe, for he was a very kind and helpful man, but he dead within the week of the arrest. Nobody could say or do nothing. Papa Joe dead and that's that.

The way Papa Joe die worry me a great deal. I wanted to leave North Sound and go in search of a job some place else. But it wasn't that easy. You see, jobs was hard to get at the time and I couldn't afford to be out of work. Another thing that make leaving hard, was that back then you would have to get permission to leave from one estate to the other. Also, my mother was having about one new baby a year and I use to work to help her out. And another reason that keep me at North Sound a little longer than I really wanted was that the planters use to show some likeness for me. They say I work fast and don't give any trouble. As I reach sixteen they move me out of the small gang and give me a raise. But I would just ask myself how long I could stay on a place where it seem there was no end to what they could do to you.

A man call Smart, of Dundun and Maul, was found dead with a piece of cane stuffed in his mouth one day in a cane field across from the pain-killer tree at North Sound. The word was he was murdered by the war-man — the militia planter by the name of Massa Denny. In my view that Denny was nothing but a killer. A violence he talk every time he open he mouth.

Now to steal the bakkra cane was a very serious thing. Dundun Smart was a known thief and he don't care if them catch he; if he got out of the jailhouse this morning, he was sure to be back this afternoon and he never hide when he thief the bakkra things. Dundun was the only man I know in all my time that would go and break a cane and eat it any place for all to see. Massa Denny use to swear to God that one day he is going to make sure Dundun stop breaking cane. Nobody saw him kill Dundun, but before Dundun's body was found, that officer was walking around the estate saying that Smart now stop eating canes. Nobody that was around when he say that have the idea that he kill Dundun, but when the news come that Dundun was found dead, people start to rumour that Massa Denny catch Dundun breaking cane and choke him dead. No magistrate come to take a look at the body — Dundun was just taken away like an animal.

As time goes by, the planters change the ways from open murder to quiet and sly means. Take poison. During my young days — and even up to now — some people always like to be in massa's company and usually would feel big if the bakkra come and offer them a piece of cake or a drink. When somebody offend against massa and massa feel that somebody must die, well that was that. A good number of our people dead of poisoning at the hands of the planters. Sometimes the planters was quick to blame it on the yellow fever. God knows they were lying on the fever. Our people also learnt the art of poisoning and a lot of people dead from that for many years in Antigua.

Strange, though, that the nega man poison his own brother; he never think that he should poison massa.

There was a young planter at North Sound called Massa McDougal. For some time I use to feel McDougal was a little better than the other bakkra, for he use to talk to the people and make joke with them from time to time and, if you ask him a favour he would grant it most of the time. One day he give to some farmers a hard lump of sugar that was found at the bottom of the molasses tank. Some weeks later, chief planter Massa Hinds chide him for this and for talking with the people. Planter never used to forget to call the names[4] of the people that make reports to them; neither have they ever kept a secret for a black man or black woman. So Massa Hinds tell young Massa McDougal the report about the molasses come from Dicky Humphreys. Then Massa McDougal hate the guts of Dicky. Near Christmas in 1895, or thereabouts, Massa McDougal give Dicky a drink of rum. Dicky didn't remember that the planter have it up for him, so he accept the drink. Anyway, there was other people around drinking massa's drink and nega was not suppose to refuse nothing from the massa. When Dicky done drink the rum, Massa McDougal cuss the hell out of him. Dicky left North Sound works the very minute, shaking and feeling shame. He worked out that week and then took ill and he dead about two months later.

McDougal boast that he is the man that shut up Dicky, for Dicky never learn to see-and-don't-see and hear-and-don't-hear. Dicky's life was long, but he was careless with it, was what McDougal told the gang. He was proud to get rid of Dicky. Him feel he did no wrong. Nobody question Massa McDougal, though. He was the law.

There was many more cases of poisoning at North Sound while I was working there, but the one that stands out most forcibly to my mind is the poisoning of Missy Friday, a young gal of nineteen.

I was just a year younger than Missy Friday and we get to be close friends because we were born on the same day. In truth and

4. The planters always named their informers.

fact, I use to want to be in love with her, but she didn't take me on. (Now I hardly lose a battle of that kind so I should say she didn't live long enough.)

Her mother have a job in Massa Hinds buff[5] as a servant and the massa make several efforts to win the love of Missy Friday. Instead she fall in love with another planter, one Massa Reynolds of Cassada Gardens. Now that love affair arouse the wrath of Hinds, but the young Missy Friday keep on accompanying her mother to work.

One day Hinds give the young lady a piece of cake. After she finish eating the cake she get ill. The massa provide the cart and we take her home to Cassada Gardens where she live with her mother. Her lover Massa Reynolds, went and got the estate doctor to attend to her. The doctor say Missy Friday was poisoned. When her mother hear that she accuse Hinds of poisoning the gal and Hinds drove the mother off the estate. And Missy Friday also say on her sick bed that she was sick from the cake Hinds give her and that he did it because she wouldn't make love with him. Well, doctors wasn't that clever in them days and Missy Friday die. There was terrible sadness amongst the people. What happen to Missy Friday made me make up my mind to leave North Sound come hell or starvation.

Massa Reynolds was feeling that because Missy Friday was a potogy[6] and his missis, that she should have the privilege to get buried at St. George's churchyard. We also believe she was going to St. George's, but no such thing. The white minister refused to have anything to do with the funeral and she was buried instead at Blizzard Estate, not far away.

Murder was not all the bakkra have to use against us. Back then there was two magistrates courts in that part of the island, one at English harbour and the other at Parham. The magistrates also use to go around the estates on every other Tuesday and settle cases. Now when you see the magistrate come, who have case would straighten up. Them frighten. A lot of them magistrates was planters or in the family of planters.

5. Bluff. Planters frequently built their houses on hill tops or bluffs.
6. Missy Friday was part Portuguese.

In them days a good portion of the people would go to jail for all kinds of simple things. The cat-o-nine was the worse that could happen to you in the jail-house. And if you be unruly, you would also get a 75 lb. ball locked to your waist or ankle by a chain and you would have to try and move around with it.

Back then, the jail-houses was built on wheels and they was pulled all over the island by the prisoners. Most of the people that was sent to jail from the district use to end up in them jails on wheels. They were moving prisoners: where night meet them, them sleep. Them prisoners was forced to shoot hard labour for the planters and that happen to be one of the main reasons that people get put in jail.

It seem to me that the whole jail-house thing was set up to keep us down and make sure the bakkra always have plenty workers for free. For example, the magistrates use to order a fine he very well knew you couldn't pay and then you would be off to the jail house. For sure them never make joke with that.

I will always remember some of the people close to me that get punished one way or another by the planters. There was Paul Valentine of Potters Village that was sent to jail for not showing up for work. Them planters didn't make joke with nobody. Nobody. Nega was to labour as hard as them possibly could to put money in bakkra pocket. No other interest did them have.

One Missy Burke, of All Saints, was put in jail for drinking water from the well at North Sound. Missy Burke told the magistrate that she did drink the water from the well. The sun was hot and she was thirsty. Then she begged him pardon. She got three months hard labour.

I remember Tommy Joseph, of Piggots Village, got sent to the jail house for accidentally touching the bell rope at North Sound Estate. It was near lunch time when it happened, so we went to eat. The bakkra took Tommy Joseph to the magistrate for "maliciously ringing the estate bell". He got six months in the jail and banned from putting foot on the estate compound for a year after that.

There was also what happened with the white wood tree and Maggie Prentice and her man, one Clive of Parham. Now that tree was specially planted for its hard wood, by the bakkra, to repair the cart that pull the sugar cane, the buggy and other things. It was also used to make shafts and staves for the cartwheels. The planters use to trim them trees good and make sure the branches was growing straight.

One day Maggie and Clive was charged for trespassing under a white wood tree, with the intention of stealing the wood. The way it happened was that the planters had cut the white wood and the pieces of the branches was left under the tree. When the watchman saw Maggie and Clive under the tree, he accuse them of stealing. Now they wanted to take up the leftover pieces of wood to make fire, but they didn't even have time for that because the watchman come around.

The magistrate said it was for the planters to say if them pieces of wood was useless and should be used to catch fire. Negas, he said, like to steal and the jail house was there to keep them for a while whenever they get caught. Maggie and Clive get three months hard labour.

I will never forget the closest I got to trouble during my whole life. We were pulling sugar from North Sound to Painters when we meet a group of prisoners working on the road. One of them was beckoning to me and I throw him a lump of sugar. The guard saw me, stopped the cart and yell to me he was going to lock me up. I beg him pardon and told him I didn't know that was an offense, so he warn me and give me a break. I was lucky.

If you was absent from work for whatever reason or late too often, it was jail or licks or both. Sometimes after a man did not show up for work his lady friend would take him to massa to be whipped in order for him to get back his job. Many men get whipped that way. It was humiliating, but that's the way it was. (I can't properly explain how hard, how difficult life was back then, but I would sure like for the younger generation — some don't give a damn about nothing and nobody — to share some of what I saw. I would like to rap with them.)

Often when we happen to be together, the planter in charge of the gang would gallop his horse and guide it into the group to make us scatter. Them laugh to see how we have to scamper out of the way.

One day when we have finished with dropping dung at one

field and was awaiting orders, massa come galloping the horse with the intention to scatter us. Missy Cadwell, a woman from Stoney Hill, was in the group and she was a little hard of hearing. When we run out of the way of the horse, she ran right into it and was trampled. Her knee came out of place so it gather inflammation and she couldn't stretch out the leg. After a period she die. If there was a good doctor in them days, she probably would have lived. But, what is fun for a dog is death to mongoose.[7]

And you know, even after what happen to Missy Cadwell, massa keep on running them horses at us.

The North Sound planters was members of the St. George's Anglican Church where they use to go to church regularly. The planters and them wife use to go by buggy to church, but time and time again they would use us workers instead of the horses to pull them. You see, sometimes they decide the horses should get a rest; other times massa would just be angry and wanting to put pressure on us. Normally it use to take three of us to pull the buggy and a fourth when the ground was wet.

Whether we pull the buggy or go along to attend to the horses, we couldn't stay around the church while the massa and family was inside. We would have to go and wait some distance away under a tamarind tree nearby. When massa and family was ready they would tip the bell and we would move to the door of the church to carry them back home.

In 1896 when I was nineteen, I decide then and there that I was going to leave North Sound. I didn't say nothing about it to nobody. Around that time I get a promotion to be in charge of a gang and a raise in pay. All the workers would have to take orders from me. I was the first black man to get that position at North Sound and believe you me, I earn it. I worked for long hours without pay and sometimes when I left the estate all the rest was gone. They use to call me "Flash" for I worked hard and fast.

But my mind was already made up to leave North Sound and

7. Whereas a dog enjoys chasing and capturing a mongoose, the mongoose experiences fear and death.

nobody and no pay could stop me. I went to Betty's Hope to look for a job.

I had to stay on at North Sound Estate for that year and in 1897, after the crop was finish, I went over to Duers Estate and ask the Goodwins for a job. The Goodwins knew me very well for they used to see me at North Sound when they would visit the planters there and also when they went to church at St. George's on special occasions. In that same year sometime in July, I finally put foot off North Sound Estate — praise the Lord — and went to work for the Goodwins. I didn't have to get permission from the North Sound planters to leave for the Goodwins say to me they would take care of that. Them Goodwins[8] was big people.

Now when the bakkra at North Sound find out that I was working with the Goodwins at Duers, they get angry. That mash up[9] them something, for the Goodwins raid them of Flash.

Man, let me tell you, our people pass through some very perilous times in them days, but specially at North Sound. In the seven years that I work at North Sound black people get less respect from the English planter than what the beasts of the field get. Men and women was tortured and killed like stray dogs. If slavery time was worse, how did our people survive? I still thank God I never fall victim at North Sound. I always have the belief that if I could get out of North Sound without a mark I would go back home to God without a mark on my body.

8. R.S.D. Goodwin, one-time chief planter, council member and local historian. He appears again in later chapters.
9. Annoyed them a great deal.

St. George's Church built in 1735: the church where blacks were not allowed to worship during slavery. Shortly after slavery ended, blacks were allowed to worship in the church but were seated separately from whites. The practice continued well in the twentieth century.

The blacksmith shop: the blacksmith trade was one of the most popular trades in earlier times.

Jonas Tower: built during slavery, this historical monument still stands on Jonas estate where Samuel "Papa Sammy" Smith was born.

The dagger stalk tree.

Old Plantation House in ruin. Its occupants were called "Nega house people".

Governor Feinnes: Governor of Antigua 1921-1929. He tried to improve water supply, roads and medical care. Popularly known for initiating the building of the Fiennes Institute or old age house.

Papa Sammy walking to church on his 105th birthday.

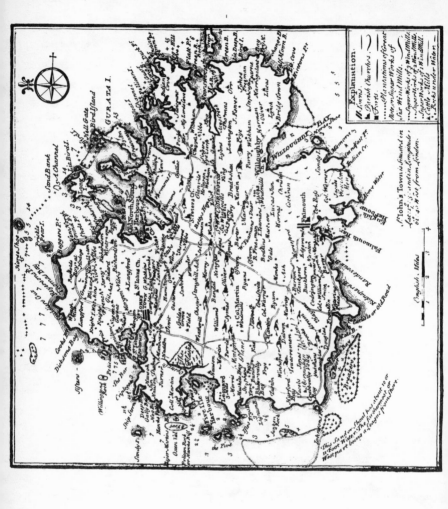

18th century map of Antigua before villages were formed.

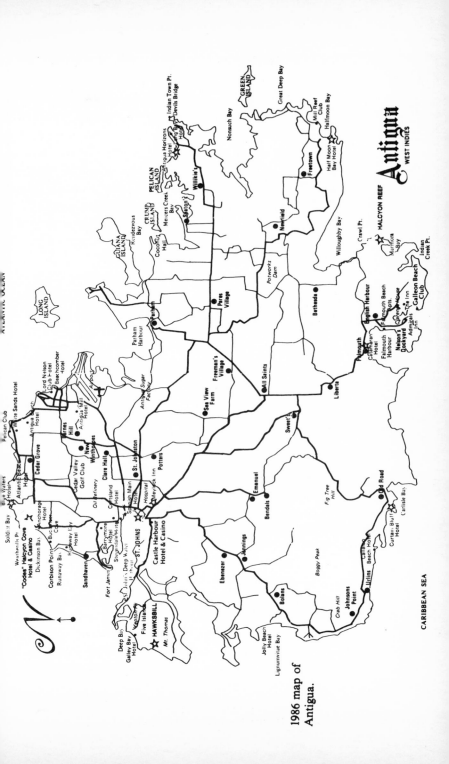

1986 map of Antigua.

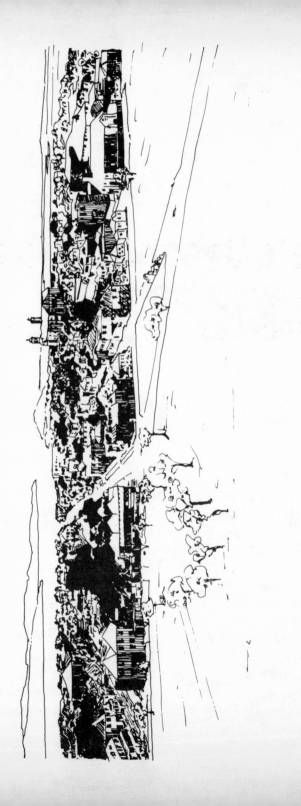

St. John's, Antigua, 1898, as described by Samuel "Papa Sammy" Smith.

5

Life's Ups and Downs:
God Was With Me All the Way

In the name of the Lord I finally leave North Sound. At long last I get to be at ease with myself, for after seven perilous years I escape that place without a mark.

That was no easy luck for — never mind how good a nega man try to be back then — it did not take plenty for the bakkra to treat him the same as the other negas. Mark you, I never get the impression that just because I left North Sound I would be out of danger. Life in them days did not permit that, but worse could not be anywhere else.

At that time nearly every nega wanted to work at Betty's Hope. Betty was the largest estate on the island and it would have a good amount of work while the others would have very little — particularly in the dull season[1] — for Betty was responsible to carry out the repairs on the mills and other equipment for some of the other estates. It also had two mills at

1. After the harvest.

the time and was used to ground the canes for the other estates that have no mill.

The workshop at Betty was second to none on the island and the best tradesmen of all kinds was there. Blacksmith service was one of the most important things back then and no place could touch Betty's Hope. Coopering[2] and tannering[3] was also important back then and old Betty was very capable in them things too. I badly want to get into the workshop there for I wanted a chance to learn to be a cooper or a blacksmith, any chance I got I would take. The big man for the estate promise me a job in the workshop and in my early days at Duers, I was waiting for a call. That call never come, so I settled in at Duers.

At Duers my main job was to hold plough. I would have to control the plough while the cattle would pull it through the fields. The animals travel much slower when we close plough[4] than when the second cut was taken or the banking[5] was done. The slowness was due to the fact that the land was always tighter[6] for the first cut. That part of the job was less harassing. At other times, though, the animals use to move much quicker and that was tiresome. We use to always find songs to sing when we was working in the boiling sun to keep our minds off the task and lessen the pressure. The singing also keep the animals in some control. One of the song we use to sing go like this:

> Massa say if I serve him when I die
> A gonna go to heaven when I die
> Serve him at the very best
> Heaven me portion when I die
> Wo, wo, wo, wo
> Heaven me portion when I die.

The planters was very well versed on what to do to get the best yields out of the particular fields. Each was plough according to where it was and how it would drain — the drainage was a special part of the ploughing operation.

2. Barrel making and repairing.
3. Tanning hides.
4. The first ploughing.
5. Sugar cane is planted in the furrows between banked soil.
6. Harder to plough.

One of my jobs was to make sure the ploughing was done properly and on time. It was tiresome to keep moving up and down from one end of the field to the other. We hardly would have a break from morning till night, keeping pace behind the plough for twelve hours and more each day. We would have to be always on the alert to make sure that the plough was kept in control and we would get a lot of box-bout[7] from the cattle plough, for Antigua land no level and the dry spells make it plenty hard to plough and that make the work much harder for us.

The planters knew how tiresome ploughing was, but them have more feeling for the cattle and them than them have for nega people. In truth and fact, the bakkra never joke with the proper care and treatment of the animals. They lay down some very strict rules to protect them that every ploughman have to obey to the proper. No cattle could pull plough for more than three half days a week. If six cattle was yoked this morning, another six should be yoked this afternoon. The set that start work from Monday, done work by Wednesday. The other set will take the place from Thursday to Saturday. No animal must be yoked if hurt or sick, no matter how them botheration. If you whale any of them, the magistrate wouldn't even want to see you.[9] The nega man would never escape jail.

Nega man would have to find himself behind that plough even if sick. Plenty man they drop down dead behind plough because they couldn't stay home when sick. Massa hardly believe when them talk. It was an offence to even complain, so workers was afraid to let massa know they couldn't make it. Neither was there half days for us. Sick or well, we were forced to hold that plough. I held plough for years and never slow up. I was lucky I was never sick.

I didn't even get a headache. When the sun was hot I would put cattle tongue leaves under my hat to keep my head cool.

7. The plough was hard to control.
8. A jail sentence would result.
9. The worker would get taken to court and sentenced, regardless of extenuating circumstances.

That hat was a date hat with a big rim. Almost all of us that worked the estates use to wear that kind of hat. The big rims was to protect our faces from the sun and to give us some shelter from drizzle rain. (Them hats was made by the people of Liberta Village, the biggest village in the island and one of the most fruitful. Liberta Village hat makers use to travel all around Antigua selling, and at the same time taking in new orders. Most of the people from Liberta could earn a living without working directly with the plantation, for them hats was in great demand. My mother use to tell me how the slaves from the village learnt to plait the hats and bags from the wife of an English slave owner by the name of Missy Wycomb. Wycomb, she use to tell me, got the knowledge from a house slave she have living with her from Madeira. I believe that the Africans reached Antigua with some skills too, but them couldn't do anything except to work in the sugar cane fields. They couldn't teach nobody. There wasn't any time for that.)

I did everything and anything on the estate and in quick time I develop a good, good relationship with the Goodwin family — not only Massa Affie, my boss at Duers — but all the Goodwins, them that live at Collins Estate as well as Guyanas. The Goodwins was the big shots in Antigua at the time. So much that at one time it appears that the governor was not bigger than R.S.D. Goodwin. You see, R.S.D. was chief planter, councillor, historian and teacher. A big man.

I don't think there was one planter back then that didn't at some time or the other abuse the nega physically. When I put the way things was at North Sound up against the attitude of the Goodwins, I have to say that the Goodwins was good people, but they were not all guiltless. The Goodwins was well known for putting them dogs on negas when they fall out with them. When Massa Affie would get vex with you, you couldn't cross them estate for the dogs would be put on you and after that the magistrate would deal with you for trespassing.

Whatever the Antigua planters would have against the nega — and I know that all was not the same — they sure have one thing in common when it come to paying black people that work for them. All of them believe that we must work for nothing.

That was the case when I start to work and it was the same when I went on pension seventy-two years later.

Massa like to see man work like them crazy, so at Duers, just as at North Sound, I was the first to be on the estate in the morning and last to leave at nights. The Goodwins was quick to recognize my worth. They start to take me into them house. What a thing, there was jealousy over me between them. R.S.D. Goodwin want Affie to send me over to them. This Affie would do sparingly.

But the best the Goodwins did was to open up their books to me. Duers was the first place I get in contact with so many books. They use to teach me to read and understand what I read. I get to know that there was such a thing call a dictionary. And whenever the Goodwins was finished with the newspaper they would give them to me. For many years I use to be the only man in village that was reading the newspapers regularly.

I learnt enough that I could help my people in the village at the night schools. And whenever somebody would have a name that was difficult to spell, I would take it to the Goodwins and they would tell me how to spell it. Few people in my day got that kind of privilege. I would then go back to the night school the next night and teach it to the villagers. I was very thankful then, and I am now glad that I was able to help my people to learn to read.

Though I was the general boy for the Goodwin family, Affie was my boss. As time pass, they would let me into some other things that I never thought was possible. Poor-me-poor-fellow could go in and out of the Great House. That was the Goodwin's original home that they built at Collins Estate in 1813. In my time it was the home of R.S.D. and Mrs. Goodwin. The garden there was the most beautiful in Antigua and at the entrance these words was written in bold prints:

> The kiss of the sun for pardon,
> The song of the birds for mirth
> God is nearer one's heart in a garden
> Than anywhere else on earth.

Any new planter reaching the island would make sure that he make a visit to that place.

The planters had the habit to use the place as the second

Council Chamber and it seem to me that that Council Chamber was just as powerful as the Governor-in-Council. It was also the place where they use to go to discuss serious matters and the place where some of the most fancy feasts was held. In my time the governor would usually hold a feast every January for the members of Council. That would be followed by the Councillors' Feast at the Great House just before the crop start. No governor or other feast could touch that, the way planters and them friends would live it up.

It was there I get to know people like L.I. Henzel, the Codmans, the Maginleys, W.O. McDonald, Scott Johnson, and many others.[10] The Great House was the first place I saw Magistrate Athill.[11] That sure surprise me. He was the first black guest I see there.

We wouldn't mind them have feast every day, simply because after the feasting we would make hay with them leftovers. Man sure use to feel big when he have massa leftovers to carry home. The governors use to also make regular weekend visits at the Great House and the Goodwins — mostly R.S.D. and his wife — use to pay back visits. At them times I would mainly take care of the buggy. I was their all-in-all.

On Christmas Eve 1898 the Goodwins carry me to town with them. I was twenty-one years old, but up to then, I never see St. John's. It was a big day in my life. Most of the black people at the time live years, dead and never put foot there. When we reach the city I was frightened and if they had sent me any distance that particular day I would get lost for sure. Buggies was all over the place. A lot of white people was shopping. There was just a few blacks around — nothing to speak about — and most of them was doing duties like I was doing. The planters was all over the place, going all out to get ready for Christmas day.

Sometime after 5:00 or 6:00 p.m. that day, the shoppers start to leave town and the buggies was behind each other going out of St. John's. We had company right up to Sandersons. I remember sharing cakes and sweets that I got from the Goodwins to my

10. Wealthy white estate owners.
11. The first black magistrate in Antigua.

family. It was my best Christmas so far.

When Old Year's Day[12] come I was back with the Goodwins in town again. I could not believe it: I was visiting the city twice in one week. That time it was the whole Goodwin family that went. The reason why all of them was in town was to ring out the Old Year and with the Old Year's Night service at Big Church and bring in the new with feasting and merriment.

We reach town earlier than on Christmas Eve and the Goodwins go and do a little shopping and then go to sleep. After church my massas would go from one party to the next till morning. (I don't think that plenty people can ever afford to live that life the planters use to live. Most of them use to overeat and they would have some enormous bellies. In truth and fact, some of them bellies use to hang over the horse saddles, but they sure was proud of the big bellies. They was also mostly bald-headed so people use to say anybody with bald head have money.) But poor me can't sleep. I have to see how town tap.[13] My confidence start to grow for after all, it was the second time around.

I start to cover the whole place, trying to remember the streets, but it was hard for me to remember all I wanted to. I was still excited, but not as much as the first time.

New Year's Day 1899 was the first New Year's Day I spent in town. It was my twenty-second birthday and my massas give me a big cake, the usual birthday gift. Since I start working with them they never miss out on that. I could hardly believe my eyes when I look out on that New Year's Day: all the music, the dancing, the masquerading clowns and the whole New Year's jump up[14] was white people. The English massas and them family was enjoying themself. Sometime later the Goodwins tell me that the merry makers was Scotchmen and they were the ones that brought Christmas celebration to Antigua.

After a time the Goodwins turn over the city run to me, and since I also use to have to go almost everywhere with them, I get to know the city well. I remember the layout of the place to this

12. New Year's Eve.
13. See what St. John's was like.
14. Festivities.

day. The city fathers called the eastern boundary line of St. John's, East Street, the northern was North Street and the southern, South Street. East Street at the top of the town run from North to South. North and South streets would stretch from top of East Street to the sea front on the west side. Between North and South Streets there was eight streets running in the same direction.

In addition to East Street there was three other streets running north to south. The main street — the same street that is now called Market Street — was called Scotch Row back then because it was the business centre and all the business on both sides of it stretching from South Street at the southern end to Newgate Street in the north use to belong to Scotchmen. (The Scotchmen had most of the business in Antigua for many years.)

The streets was made with stones mixed with sand and use to have a brown appearance. The stones was taken from the quarry opposite St. Johnson's Village and the sand use to come from the beaches. The street now called Factory Road use to be Long Street and it would divide St. Johnson's Village from the quarry. On East Street, between Nevis and Tanner Streets, was a large pond — Country Pond — that takes the water that runs off the hill overlooking the town. That water wasn't for drinking.

The Cathedral with its two steeples almost frighten me when I saw it first and it seem to me that the feeling was usual for the time. It was the big symbol of English power. The planters use to call it Big Church and it was big in name and nature. It sits on the rising at the crossroads of Church Street and Temple Street and the steeples could be seen from just about any direction. Church Street runs from east to west, through the east and west gates of the property. And Temple Street run through the North and South doors of the Church building.

At the south gate there's two statues. Back then, we use to call them Adam and Eve, but I think they find a new name for them now.

Just to the west of the church, in front of the gates, was the public market — just an open place with some trees around the area. Not even a shed. The church and the trees would shade the sun and help to keep the place cool.

Just a little away from the market on Church Street in an open space under a big mahogany tree was the old slave market where the bakkra use to sell our generations. That mahogany tree had hooks and spikes in it. After slavery end, Delos Martin, a Scotchman built a business place just west of it and that would block the view of the courthouse at the corner of Scotch Row and Church Street.

The upper room of the courthouse was the Council and just north of the courthouse was the gun house. At the bottom of High and St. Mary's Streets was the Queen's Warehouse. Down that area always use to be busy.

On the eastern side of the Cathedral — just inside the city limit — was the Governor's house. It was destroyed in 1710 when the planters killed Governor Parkes and it wasn't put up again till 1800. A few yards outside the city limit on the east of the Governor's house was an open space we use to call Victoria Park. Now it's called the Recreation Ground.

Almost just east of that was the hospital and to the south side of the hospital was the prison.

The prison there now was put up in 1735. I was told that it wasn't built for the slaves. In the first place, the slaves was in prison already. The prison was for anybody that would get captured trying to invade the island.

The Parham Road would divide the hospital on the south from the place we call Palmer Jelly on the north.

The little hill at the head of the city — the one in a straight line with High and St. Mary's streets — was called Gibbet's Hill. It was the place where the open gallow was built — close to what is now call the Botanical Gardens — but the slaves use to call it Dribbet House. The open gallows was like the frame of a house. Them gallows would have three or four planks overhead. The slaves use to be tied with rope at the neck or shoulders, around the waist, or any part of the body for that matter. They was then pulled up and tie to the overhead planks and they would be left there to swing. A portion of food would be left in front of them, but that food was to let the slaves see it and not reach it. They were made to swing there till they dead. Nowadays, when you want to show how harsh you want to deal with somebody, you say, "Me go kill you". Back then we use to say, "Me go gibbet you".

The Scotchmen use to have them place of worship near Gibbet's Hill. It was call Scotch Kert[15] but it was blown down in the hurricane of 1871 and only the gallows and some trees remain on the hill. The gallows was not taken down till when Haynes Smith get to be Governor of Antigua.

The early planters use to live in mortal fear of hurricanes and typhoons, so they would plant mahogany trees for protection. They had them around East Street to mark the first defense line of the city. The trees further east called the second defense line and they use to plant trees around Government House as a means of defense for the Governor. So too, was the trees on the estates and at other places.

Another famous street in St. John's was Pope's Head Street where the English people would cut the head off the image of the Pope every year and burn it. That's how the street got its name. It runs into Newgate Street from the north.

On the northern side of upper Newgate Street was Mico College, the place that the Moravians would use to train some of their ministers. A little below the college on the same street was the Mico School, a mixed school[16] that the Moravians use to operate. That school also use to be the headquarters of the debating society the Moravians set up a little after the turn of the century. That place use to do a tremendous job. It taught the big portion of us how to be the massa of the language and how to debate.

Further south of Mico College, on St. John's and St. George's streets, was the big Moravian Church and the famous Spring Gardens Seminary.

The Rev. Westerby, a Moravian minister, set up the seminary in 1841. The bishop or minister was first living in Sea View Farm where he was in charge of the Lebanon Moravian Church. It was there he started training teachers: all of them gals. He later went to St. John's where he make great efforts to educate the people

15. Scotch Kirk or Scotch Church.
16. Racially mixed.

and built one of the most important institutions in Antigua.[17]
The Seminary was the training school for the advanced teachers
in the Caribbean so the Moravians was very proud of it.

I can remember a time ago there was a very popular song on
the seminary. It goes something like this, "Me send me daughter
a seminary, now she come back with a big fat belly". A man by
the name of John Quarkoo use to sing for money and one day he
was singing this song to some people in town when a Moravian
parson by the name of H.B. Hutton was passing by and he hear
Quarkoo. That parson get very angry. He told singer Quarkoo
that he, the parson, would never allow him or anybody to
disgrace the seminary that has been doing so much good for the
people of Antigua and the West Indies. He then took Quarkoo
to court. At the sitting, the magistrate share the same view as the
parson and he sent old Quarkoo to jail for six months.

The Methodist was a little late in coming here. The Anglicans
and the Moravians reached Antigua long before the John
Wesley people. Nathaniel Gilbert was the first Methodist to
reach here, in 1759, or so I hear. He started to preach the
Methodist religion at the eastern part of the island and the place
is known as Gilbert's Estate. R.S.D. Goodwin use to talk about
the famous Gilbert steps where Methodism start in the New
World.

At upper St. Mary's Street was Coke College, the Methodist
school for training their ministers. The Methodist later rented
out the building to the Colonial Office. The plan for the building
of the large Methodist Church that is on St. Mary's and Redcliffe
streets stayed in the Colonial Office for well over fifty years
before the Methodists get permission to put it up. They use to go
and have their worship at a small church in South and Temple
streets.

At the south entrance to St. John's was the national burying
ground. We use to call it Eve's Garden. Except for the
Anglicans, all the white people use to bury there. The Anglicans
use to bury in the cathedral churchyard and the poor black negas
was bury separately at Lady Nugent near Sutherland Heights on

17. The Moravian Seminary, no longer in existence.

the Parham Road. You see, the white people was very particular about where they get buried. Their dead was not to mix with poor people. Me, I always have the feeling that all dead be the same, but back then the English massas sure didn't think so. They show the clear belief that a white dead was always better than a black dead.

I remember Col. Cotton — he was owner of Gambles Estate and a war man like my boss Affie Goodwin — get crippled in the Boer's War. The colonel was the first man I ever see knit like a granny. He give a piece of his estate to be the national cemetary. Now sugar cane fields in them days was known by numbers, and the field the colonel give have the name Number Ten, so we use to call the cemetary Number Ten. The bakkra then stop burying them dead at Eve's Garden and at the Anglican churchyard, but Lady Nugent was still for we.

I remember how St. John's city was always busy, how something was always going on there. When Council was meeting, the members use to show off in they frill shirts and scissors-point coats and them top hats. Them boast for so.[18] I remember there was other times when the drums would sound in the city. Now that was real excitement and it was the usual for the people to flock around the court to hear. The officer would get out the courthouse and beat them drums and then say what it was he have to say. Then he would beat them drums again and say "God save the Queen!" Everybody was always wanting to know what make drum roll for drums no roll for joke. Drum always was the signal that serious business was taking place. Sometimes it mean that war break out some place or them pass some funny law or things like flour and rice gone up. Drums also roll when them read the Riot Act.

The St. John's harbour get to be very busy when the businessmen decide to transfer them business from Parham to St. John's around the turn of the century. Parham was a seaport town in the northeast part of the island and it use to be pretty busy, but the big businessmen like McDonald, Brysons and Dews have the feeling that the Port of St. John's was much better

18. They were bombastic.

for trade. It was a change that leave Parham dead, but it bring a lot of life to St. John's harbour.

The governor at the time of the change was Haynes Smith. St. John's harbour was very shallow so Gov. Smith — the first governor to live permanently at the governor's official house[19] — bought a dredge to dredge it out. That help a bit but not enough to let big ships come close up. Now the English government was not happy over the amount of money that he was spending to buy that dredge and the English called the governor home to England to explain why he have to spend so much money on the harbour.

One of the reasons why the harbour could not be dredge deep enough to let the big ships to dock right up was because care have to be taken to make sure that Ballas Bank — a natural ridge that break the water force outside of the mouth of the harbour and that keep the harbour calm usually — didn't get damage. Ballas Bank was well needed to protect the city from heavy flooding and swells. If the bank would be removed the city would be open to terrific flooding, particularly in times of hurricanes.

I remember how the island use to suffer from drought almost every year and how several wells was dug in and around the city to supply the water. English-made hand pumps was what they used to draw the water from the wells back then and the place was punched with wells all over: one on St. Mary's and Cross streets and one on Nevis Street; another on Scotch Row and St. Mary's that was belonging to the Scotch businessman by the name of David Tory.

And almost every plantation too would have its springs or wells, but they would use the fanmill to pump out the water. General Spring — the biggest one and the one the slaves use to call Genal Spring — was at North Sound. That spring was never out of water and use to be the main supply in the dry season. At North Sound, too, there was the Hundred Steps Spring with a grip on every other step to make it safe for you when you would have to go down in the spring from time to time to clean it out.

19. Government House.

Provided the bottom was clear, that spring was always full of water.

Ottos Dam — on what is now called Camacho's Avenue, or Dam Gutter as it was back then — was another supply of water to St. John's in the times of drought, but Ottos Estate owners never did like to give the city people the water. Sometimes the governor have to dip mouth in there for them to get the water.[20] St. John's also use to get water from a reservoir that was up on Gray's Hill. The reservoir was built by Governor Sir Stephen Hill.

People use to go up on top of Gray's Hill to watch the sunset. Except for the sea at the western end of the town, there was sugar cane fields all around. The green surroundings use to mix with the brownishy look of the town and when the sun use to sink on the open ocean, it was very pleasant. In December it use to be even more beautiful, for some of the fields would have harra.[21] Plenty white people use to go up there to Gray's Hill just to watch the sunset, but me, I use to like to watch it from between Clarke's Hill and Briggins Road and I still think that view was the better.

To the north, near the village of Cedar Grove, there was a large cave that I hear use to be the home of some of the people that live in the island before Columbus. Affie Goodwin use to tell me how Columbus and his men overpower them people, took away their tools and other important things out of the cave and carried them things to Spain. He said that his history told him that Columbus' landing on Antigua wasn't all that easy, that there was strong resistance.

That Affie Goodwin have a lot of faith but he was afraid to go too far down into the cave. Inside was dark and you would have to light lamp to see where you was going. I always felt the presence of somebody whenever I happen to visit that cave and it appear that, that was the feeling of all them that happen to go there, at least in my time.

South of the cave is St. Maria Hill and that place is suppose to

20. The governor had to intervene so that the city would have access to the water at Ottos Estate.
21. Some of the cane fields would be in bloom.

be the first thing inside Antigua that was name by Columbus. I hear that Columbus enter Antigua from the north and that the hill was the first thing he saw. There's several holes a little way from the top of the hill that the people that live here before Columbus used to use as shelter. Affie Goodwin use to like to explore around there and I climbed St. Maria Hill a few times with him. I also use to hear that the Barbudan fishermen would use the hill as a mark when they would be sailing between Antigua and Barbuda.

To the east of St. Maria Hill is Mount Joshua, called after the planter that had the estate there. In that same area, but further east, was Thibou Jarvis Estate. Thibou was a member of Council and well known for having a lot of weight with the governors. His family built the famous Massa Grave. The planters at Thibou Jarvis Estate use to say that massa grave was better than those at Big Church.

North of the cave was the Boon's Chair, at the tip of Boon's Point, where the early people carve out seats in the rock that was overlooking the sea. It was an exciting thing to sit in the chairs with the ocean lashing below. The story was that before you could sit in the chair, you would have to make the sign of the cross and pay some money or you would be suddenly forced out of that chair and into the ocean by a spirit, so whenever I follow Affie Goodwin to sit in the chairs, we would make the sign of the cross and pay a penny or two.

The Antiguan Communication Centre was on the south side of the island, but long before telephone and them things come in, Bolans Police Station was the communication house. They use to stay there and send them messages to the other islands. R.S.D. use to tell me they would use a light as the code, so Monsterrat would pick up the signal and send it on to St. Kitts and so on.

The first cable office and telephone exchange was in High Street with the cable at the top of the street and the telephone at the corner of High and Corn Alley. I think that cable and telephone come in just before World War I start.

I don't remember the exact time electric light came to Antigua, but it was brought here by the firm of McDonald and Company. Jack McDonald went and studied the light business in England and when he get back here he put up a small electric plant. We use to call him "Electric Jack". There wasn't much light to speak about, though. It was only put on on Saturday nights and in part of just one street, that just happen to be St. Mary's where the McDonald's was living. The business places and the planters used to use the hurricane lamps. The hurricane lamps could stand up very well during stormy times, and because of that it was of great use to them.

In the early days, quite a lot of people use to live in the south of the island. From Yorks right through to Heat's Bay was thick with all kinds of people. My grandmother use to tell me how many different races live along the seashore in that area. She use to say that people think that it was the Englishman and slaves alone live in Antigua, but that wasn't so. With the English, you use to have the Germans, Irish, Portuguese, Chinese and so on. The Portuguese was very late to reach here for they come after slavery end, but the Germans, the Irish and the rest was here well before slavery end.

Massa Shan, one of the most famous slave massas, got permission in 1846 to bring the Portuguese as indentured workers. The Peking Chinese and some other Chinese reach here from Shanghai — help us to get rid of the kooka bendals, for they was the first to build pit latrines in Antigua. The last Chinese man I know — he was a government pensioner for some time — was the one that use to lay out some of the side walks in St. John's.

The southern part of Antigua was also famous for the sea robbers because the bakkra in that area was very rich. Many years ago the first bank to be in Antigua was at Yorks, and also the first gallows was built there. I hear that slaves use to be gibbeted in that same area. People use to say that the Yorks planters have the custom to bury money in blood, all over the place. I suppose that would be before any banks was put up.

I don't know when the banks was put up in the city, but it seem to me the first one was the Colonial Bank, north of the police station on Bank Alley. The money was different back then, too. Some was of brass metal and some of silver. The farthing, halfpenny and penny was of brass. Them also have threepence and sixpence pieces, the shilling piece and the two-and-sixpence piece that they use to call a half-crown. From the threepence to the five shilling piece was made of silver. When the paper money come in — just the other day, around 1912 or thereabout — nobody want them at all.

Some people use to say that a human life have to be taken where money was buried. The people in the early days also have the practice to build on money, that a certain amount of money have to be placed at one of the pillars of anything that was being put up. My mother told me that the tower at Heat's Bay was built on pieces of gold. She also use to tell about how a good piece of money was in the ground at Jolly Hill, but the owner never would allow nobody to visit or even take a walk across Jolly Hill for he was afraid that the jumbie[22] that was guarding the money would tell where it was.

My mother also would tell me how the slave massa at Willoughby Bay — one of the richest areas to be found in all the land — was well known for the practice of putting money or some gold in the foundations of buildings. That place was like a city by itself, for they would do what they like there. It was like that place was separate from the rest of the island. It have its own seaport and cathedral.

The old slave massas of Willoughby Bay, Mamora Bay and Nelson's Dockyard use to link together. My mother would tell me how they have a way of killing slaves, that was to tie the hands and feet to a tree and drive a ten penny nail in the head. She use to call Willoughby Bay the Sodom and Gomorrah of Antigua, the place where they use to commit every evil deed under the sun. They actually carry on slavery there well after it was suppose to end in 1834, for the Englishmen at Dockyard use to sell them slaves up to 1843. Slavery actually come to an end there when the big earthquake of 1843 destroy the church and almost all the buildings. Nobody live there from that time. That church is all covered over with trees now and so too are the other buildings. Willoughby Bay and Nelson's Dockyard was also known for rape and murder on young and old slaves alike.

22. Spirit or ghost.

Nelson's Dockyard had the best slave branding shop in Antigua. My mother said they never killed a slave from branding there. The shop was closed in 1826.

People use to say that the south was the most fruitful part of Antigua. I can't say much on that, but what I do know is the most snakes was found there. I think that I am one of the few people still around today that ever saw snakes in Antigua. Plenty snakes was here for sure, but every bully have them cooler[23] and mongoose is surely the cooler for snakes. Not one around now for mongoose kill them all out.

The highest hill in the land — Boggy Peak — is also in the south. I wonder if it is called so because the official transport of the land use to be the buggy?

About five miles east of St. John's is the centre of the island at a spot on the hill now known as Clarke's Hill. Back then it was call Centre Hill, for about half mile east of the tee road[24] at the hill is the exact centre of Antigua. The centre was marked by a big stone — put in the middle of the road — about three feet long by about three feet wide and about eight inches thick. The surveyors carved out the crown and the date on that spot.

Very close by that spot is the Bear Bob Tree, the tree with the largest trunk on the island. My mother use to say it was the Devil Tree for all sorts of crimes use to take place there. Every now and then somebody would be found there either with them head bust or throat cut. Some people use to call it the Place of Wickedness and use to say that the tree was on the grave of Bob Stonny Hill Ashe.[25]

The Bear Bob Tree also use to mark the place where the slave market was. On Tuesday the slaves for sale or swap was taken there. Later on the market was move to another tree about 400 yards east of the Bear Bob tree. That second tree is suppose to be the first mahogany tree on the east side of Grandy Pond. A slave by the name of Grandy Two happen to die at that tree while she

23. Every bully meets his match.
24. A primary road shaped like a T.
25. Bob "Stonny" Hill Ashe was a planter who vowed no stones would be placed over his grave.

was up for sale and the pond take its name after her. That tree and that pond is still there.

On the north, a little way east of the tee road, is a gulley about three-quarters of a mile long running from south to north. In my day we use to call it the Stoney Hill Gulley. R.S.D. said that that was the place where the slaves meet and plan the revolt in 1736. I belive no nega should forget that place. The first time I get to know the spot was in 1904 when the Goodwins and Lord Strickland, governor of Antigua at the time, visited the spot. Some slave let out the secret and the revolt didn't get to start. A good number of slaves was tortured to force them to carry news. They called names that was never involved, and once a name was called, that person was killed. I hear it was after the slaves try and revolt that the slave massas of the land say, "Kill or be killed". Slaves couldn't even put foot off the plantation after that. (It seem to me that slavery force the slaves to become news carriers and traitors on their own people and me think we still have this problem going on up to now.)

The Goodwins know plenty of what happen at the Stoney Hill Gulley. He use to say that slave go there to worship them King and them African God. They would dance around fire, drink wine and inhale the smoke from the roasted cashew nuts. The Goodwins use to say that after slavery end hardly anyone remember the spot. Me never hear of it until the Goodwins took Lord Strickland at the spot. Tell you the truth me never hear anybody else talk of it but the Goodwins.

A little away from the gulley — was the spot where almost all the negas that was killed at North Sound, Blackman's and Jonas was buried. After I get to know the spot, I never like to pass that way because of the sad memories it bring back.

That place was very hard and stony, a spot the planters and them couldn't use to grow sugar cane. Black people couldn't use massa good land to bury our dead and the church have nothing to do with them kind of dead body anyway. That place so hard that man could hardly dig grave there, so the graves have to be shallow and the massa use to make sure they give us white lime to rotten the body away quickly. People use to have to pile stones on top of the graves, they were so shallow. Back then them hardly write down nega people name when them born and it would be even worse when them dead.

A little south away from Centre Hill is the Montula Burial Ground. Some massas around there use to make the slaves walk to the burial ground and dig their own graves. Then they kill them right there. If somebody bothers you in them days, you would say, "If you bother me, you won't even get to walk the last mile to Montula".

Massa George Goodwin, father of Affie Goodwin, use to talk a lot. He use to tell me how his family come to Antigua at the time the first set of mill towers was built in the year 1671 or so.

In the old days almost everybody use to say that the best tradesmen was usually from the villages of Willikies and Freetown and the Goodwins always use to tell me that these people did most of the work on the sugar mill towers. They was built over two hundred years ago by the Piggots of northern Ireland.

But no nega was to know the secret of the mixture of the white lime that they use to build the towers. If ever the bakkra believe that a nega was having the least idea of how the mixture was made up, he would be a dead man when the job was done. The secret of how them mix the limestone remain everlasting secret up to this day. I know that they used to use a thing from Monsterrat that they call "trickle" and they also put in lime.

And particular care was taken to make sure that the secret of the mixture didn't get out after slavery end. R.S.D. use to say if Antiguans did ever get to know the secret of the mixture there would be no wattle and daub house in the country. And for sure, that mixture with flinstones would be capital to build house. (The Antiguan tradesmen use to try to build houses with flintstone and white lime but them houses didn't last too long. It sure would be looking good though, if they did succeed in knowing the mixture.)

Old George also use to say how the bulk of the slaves come to the island after the French occupy it in 1666-1667.

Between the villages of Willikies and Seatons was the famous Parson Maules Estate that was surrounded by Grant and Dundun plantations. The few French families that didn't leave

Antigua after the French give up the land use to live at Parson Maules and around there. I hear a lot of Arawaks use to live around there too. The Goodwin family use to have a lot of ancient tools and other things that was found there.

The slave massas at Parson Maules was like the others, full of rage at the slave rebellion in 1736. The slaves saw living hell for the Parson Maules bakkra have two dungeons, the Torturer and Bump-off.

The Bump-off dungeon was blown down by the hurricane of 1871, but the one they use to call the Torturer is still there. Bump-off Dungeon had a hole in the roof and a hangman's rope run freely through that hole. A big bump was on the rope to keep it from running right through. They use to tie a slave to be bumped-off at the end of the rope with just enough length to keep that slave swinging till death. The slaves was tied from the foot, the neck, or any part of the body the massa choose.

In the Torturer, the massa would control the amount of air and light. How much you suffer depend on how tight he plug the draft and the time you have to stay in there. Some people would die in there. What a terrible way the massas at Parson Maules use to treat the slaves!

The bakkras there use to brag that the system give them the maximum production and old George Goodwin use to say that Parson Maules have more suicide than the other estates. He also use to tell me though things was tough in my time, no tongue can tell the suffering of the slaves. He let me know that Major Hole, a big planter and councillor, have some information on the way the slaves was treated at Parson Maules and on the island generally, but the major have to make oath to Gov. Freeston that he will not publish them.

Tobacco use to grow all over the land until recently and Massa George use to talk about how the English try tobacco first but that it was not making any money. Antigua, he said, was the last island to kick off its sugar processing and that was because of the lack of water. He said Antigua was even abandoned for about 140 years after the landing of Columbus for the lack of water. Many years of hard work have to be spent to prepare the land and make provisions for water.

The first sugar mill tower was put up at Clairmont on Old Road in 1670 or there about. That was a very small mill, but that area was suppose to be the best in the land so maybe that's why they start the process there. I also hear that water was not such a problem there. The famous Tom Mor Spring is on that side.

Betty's Hope — where I wanted to be a blacksmith as a boy — was built by the Codringtons in 1677. Codrington bought a large batch of slaves about that time.

Massa George Goodwin use to like to trace his generations and let you know his people was related to Queen Victoria. He was also the one that told me about how the people happen to start making the clay coal pot. You see, the early people here didn't have the knowledge of making coal pots. They used to use clay, but mostly to make pots to hold water. Them pots didn't last long because nobody knew the art of applying heat to the clay in them days.

About 1690 to 1700 the people of Sheerwood Sea View Farm learnt the heat process from the mill tower builders. The clay at Sea View Farm was the only kind found in the land that would get hard after the heat was put to it. I don't know of anybody that have knowledge of the time that clay was first found, but it is the general belief that the discovery was made by the early people. After the people got the knowledge they start to make pots of all kinds and descriptions and they get to be known as the king village.

That village could make almost anything for the better conveniences of the poor people. The first set of coal pots was suppose to be high off the ground and with only two holes in the arch. The use of the fireside to cook the food begin to fade out at that time. You know, that heat process was really simple — grass and fire was what it was.

At the northeastern point of Antigua, near Parham, is Guinea Island. It's some two miles long and half a mile wide and wild animals — mostly deer — use to live there. I think it's a lot cooler than Antigua. Guinea Island is separated from Antigua by a passage call The Narrows — the slaves use to call it The Naraz. You would have to take a pontoon to get you across the sixty or seventy feet to the island. Sometime before my time it was owned by three Englishmen — Byam, Nibbs, and Evanson, but nobody was living there in my time for many years, till a retired Englishman by the name of Major Hole — he was the one who was suppose to know a lot about slavery time — bought it.

Major Hole was on the Council and he appear to have sympathy for the union when it first start. He and Luther George, one of the founding members of the union, was good friends. Except for the servants, no nega could go on Guinea Island for it was the planter's paradise, the place where they would go and have most of their picnics. It get to be called "nude land" by people because the planters and their women and wives use to carry on gleeful nudeness there. In fact, a planter wasn't allowed to join the spree if he didn't get nude. The place also get called G.I. for "girl island". Some of the governors use to enjoy the spree there. The two main governors that people say have the most glee there was Hesketh Bell and Fiennes. I use to go there with the Goodwins when I was needed. My duties would keep me away from the action, but my job didn't keep me from seeing some of it from time to time.

On the east coast corner of island is the famous Devil's Bridge. Devil's Bridge was call so because a lot of slaves from neighboring estates use to go there and throw themselves overboard. That was a area of mass suicide, so people use to say the Devil have to be there. The waters around Devil's Bridge is always rough and anyone fall over the bridge never come out alive.

Nelson's Dockyard, built by Captain Del Garno, is situated on the south side of the island. Captain Del as they call him, famous chair and golden sword use to be on display at the Dockyard. I use to even sit in his chair. My mother told me Countess Masterson or Mother Catholic was a woman who use to give food to people in exchange for them to go to worship at the Catholic Church. That same woman my mother said knows who remove Captain Del's golden sword from the Dockyard display house.

The Goodwins was also good at taking famous people around the island. They took Governor Lord Strickland to visit the Holly rock, a place I was told the English use to worship before they built a church. I remember too, when the Goodwins took Lord Strickland to Holliday Hill and tell the story of the slave that was put in a barrel and roll down that hill as a form of punishment. The slave died from that punishment. I can remember how the Governor say it was a sad and painful thing to do. I also remember too that the governor meal for that day was the local food call sha-sha[26] and milk.

I think I was very lucky to be working where I was with the Goodwins, but most of our people was suffering. The exposure the Goodwins give me brought me a lot of knowledge and plenty of people get to know me because of the Goodwins. I got to know all the governors that reach the island between 1899 and 1950. And God was with me all the way.

The Collins Great House built and occupied by the Goodwins in 1813.

26. Corn bread.

Parson Maules Dungeon. More than one hundred and fifty years after slavery ended in Antigua, the Dungeon, situated between the village of Seatons and Willikies — the east side of the island stands in ruin. This historic monument was used to punish the slaves that did not produce enough work on Parson Maules estate. Light enters only through the door and when it was closed the Dungeon was "pitch dark". Air enters only through some small holes and the supply was determined by the Massa. Rats and insects would terrorize the slave that was punished.

Robert Stephen Duke Goodwin. Popularly known as R.S.D. Goodwin, was a prominent plantocrat council member, and a very influential personality of his time.

Spring Garden Seminary. Historical monument of Antigua left in ruin.

The St. John's Cathedral or Big Church, originally built in 1683, and rebuilt in 1745. The church was reserved for the colonial massas of Antigua. Blacks could only enter that church some time after slavery was abolished. The church was heavily damaged by the earthquake of 1974.

The Adonsonia Digitata or Boabab (Bear Bob) Tree: the tree with the biggest trunk in Antigua — forty feet in circumference. It is also one of the oldest trees in Antigua. It was planted three centuries ago on the grave of a prominent English planter, Bob Stonny Hill Ashe.

6

Hard Times:
Nega Even Though Them Right, Them Wrong

The years was rolling on. I was no longer a thirteen year old boy starting out at North Sound. By the time the Gunthorpes Sugar Factory started up in 1904,[1] I had done seven years hard work at Duers and seven at North Sound. Fourteen years of my young work life had already gone.

Gradually land got to be available and I got a piece of land to work. Along with sugar cane, I use to plant some food. Back then we use to have to work half-land. Now when the bakkra talk of half-land, it did not mean the half we learnt at school. Their half meant that if the nega plant three rows of potatoes, the massa would have the right to two of them three rows. This was the case even after the sugar factory was in operation for some time, but it was still an improvement over what it use to be. In

---

1. According to Sir Francis Watts, who played a leading role in the establishment of the first central sugar factory, the Antigua Central Sugar Factory at Gunthorpes was planned in 1903 and reaped its first crop in 1905. A second central sugar factory was set about the same time at Bendals, originally part of Belvidere Estates.

this half-land business, I have to say that the Goodwins didn't apply it to me. I had the privilege to reap all what I planted.

Things was better, but still they was tough with the usual being that you only get to reap one-third of what you plant. The people start to do a thing we call "lift" to help each other. We use to work the lift in many different ways. For instance, if I have forking[2] to do, the group would come and help me fork off my piece of land. Later I would return the help. Each person in the group would return the help until everybody got their turn. The same thing happen at reaping time. I know that if it was not for the lift, we would not get a copper[3] for all the work we put in the land. It could be that a woman working around may not be able to fork or dig root, but she would help weed or pack canes, so the group would dig the roots and fork the land for her.

The other thing that help us was the throwing of box-money. "Throwing box" means that a group of people put a particular portion of money together every week and then one of the person in the group get the hand of money — what we collect every week — for the week. That would go on every week till everybody in the group get them share. If we have ten people in the group, and each hand[4] was to pay one shilling a week, the hand-of-box is ten shillings a week and the period for the box to out[5] is ten weeks. One person would always have the job to collect the money and that person would get a short — what people call a commission nowadays. A whole lot of us use to throw box, even if the hand was only a penny a week.

Money was scarce, so we use to swap our ground provisions. We'd trade potatoes, or vegetables for cassava, and so on. The swap, throwing box and working the lift was the main things that prevent us from eating each other. People was hungry and crazy to get a piece of land to work to help themselves.

I wanted a house for myself. I was big enough and I didn't want to live any longer with my mother, but she didn't want me

2. Digging, lifting and tossing the soil.
3. A penny.
4. Person.
5. Run its cycle.

to go and live by myself. One day I decide to use a hand of box-money to start building my own house.

One of the reasons why I wanted to move from under the roof of my mother was that she never would want any of my girlfriends to come home to me. She had a terrible dislike for any woman that would get too close to her sons, but me more so than the rest. I think it was because I was working more regularly than the rest and I treat her good.

When the Goodwins find out that I am building my own house, they jump in and help me. The help from them let me build the house a little bigger than I have in mind at first.

When the house was building, there was a rumour that I was building a house to get married. Now that rumour didn't come from the people in my village because at that time nobody in the village was married. It always seem to me the rumour come from the Goodwins. My mother was disturbed. I try and comfort her, but she ring hell and I couldn't convince her that I have no intention at that time to get married. She would just say that wherever smoke there, fire there. A lot of girls was around me, but I wasn't ready yet and I didn't want to upset my mother.

In 1906 I had six children within that same year, so people start to call me "Sam the Ram". The house was finish building around the same time and the Goodwins, mostly Massa Affie and family, start to encourage me to get married. I just couldn't take them on. Affie Goodwin use to go on about how I was not in Africa where one man could have many wives and the wives feed them children. He would go on about how I was in Antigua and if I don't work, the workhouse will pick me up.

During the same time a girl by the name of Isabel had just had a child for me. Her father was a top blacksmith at Betty's Hope and it was there at Betty's Hope that I met Isabel. She use to carry her father food and I use to carry my massa horse to fix the shoe.

One day I went to do the usual check with the horse and there was quite a few people there. A white man from one of the estates decide he want to get attention of the blacksmith before all the rest of the people. The blacksmith refuse to give him attention before the people that was there before. Of course, Mr.

Joseph, the blacksmith, knew that even though there was all black faces waiting except for the white man, they was all on their massa's business. I feel that, that was the thing that give the blacksmith pluck[6] to make the white man wait his turn, for in them days, nega even though them right, them still wrong. The white planter — unknowing to anybody — went for a bucket of water and down wet-up Mr. Joseph. The man get a stroke and never catch himself again.[7] A short time after Mr. Joseph dead. As was the usual, he die unto the Lord and nobody said nothing.

The blacksmith helper that work with him was glad that he catch the stroke and die for he wanted Joe's place. He told Isabel and the others at the funeral that he wasn't the cause of Joe dying, but that it's death of wilks make soldier crab get shell.[8]

Soon after, Isabel, her picknee and her mother left the land for St. Kitts. I told the Goodwins — even though it was far from what the truth was — that the woman I was going to marry went away. That keep them from talking about married for awhile, but they never give up the fight.

Of the many girl friends I had back then, there was two of them — Clara and Lou — that was very close to me. Clara was from the village of Liberta and Lou was from All Saints. In 1907 Clara had a boy-child for me and Lou was pregnant. Around then Lou father, Samuel Peters, went off to Panama[9] and Clara father to Mingo.[10]

It was customary for Clara to come and meet me at Burke's tambran tree corner. One night I work very late, so I didn't believe that Clara would be there waiting. When I reach within distance of the usual spot I saw her. She turned sideways like she was vex with me or didn't want me to touch her. I jumped off the donkey to hug her up, but what a thing! Clara vanish. The donkey immediately railed[11] in the air and I was really wondering what the dickance was going on.

6. Courage.
7. Never fully recovered.
8. One person's loss is another's gain.
9. It is possible that Mr. Peters went to Panama in search of work on the Panama Canal which was under construction at the time.
10. Santo Domingo, the capital of the Dominican Republic.
11. Reared up.

I thought Clara dead. I was wondering what to do, should I go to Liberta or make way for home? I wasn't afraid, so I decide to go to Liberta to look for Clara.

When I reach the village there she was and nothing was wrong with her. She told me — before I could say anything — that she couldn't wait any longer. I didn't want to tell her what happen for fear that she would decide not to come and meet me again, but finally I tell her. She didn't come to the tambran tree corner again. Clara didn't want what happen to me to happen to her, so I couldn't sing sweet enough to get her to come back.

Back then, you see, it was usual to see jumbie and hear ghost bawl at nights. I remember there was a bird call the come-come bird or the dead bird. Any time that bird bawl at night, a dead was sure to be in the village before the week was done.

My mother use to tell the story of the Parham Lodge Ghost. A woman by the name of Mrs. Ramsay had an uncle with a lot of money and she poison him to get the money. No sooner she killed the man, she got burnt to death in the same house over the same money. Man, she haunt the place for years, day or night.

Clara was gone, but I was not a man to lose out. I got Lou — she didn't know about what happen at the tambran tree corner — to come and meet me. She had our first child, Ann, on the last day in February in 1908. Ann was the first child for Lou and the fifteenth for me. I was thirty-one at the time.

The Goodwins — them hardly ever give up on anything — finally convince me to get married. I decide to marry Lou. When the news broke, naturally Clara get angry with me. I went to look for her at Liberta, but she close the door in my face and drove me out of the yard. She parted from me and parted for good. I haven't behold her and child up to this day. I hear she and the child went to St. Kitts.

I was under pressure, for my mother was also mad with me. I asked Massa Affie to call her and talk to her. He did and that quieted her for a while. You see, in them days, man and woman married when them old, so nega man wedding was far and few between. In fact, I doubt that the people of All Saints ever saw a nega man wedding before I get married. Back then, when the planters get married, the people on the estates use to wait for the bride and groom. By the time the couple approach the road to where they were going, the people would start to spread all kinds of flowers behind them, something the white people always liked. When nega start to get married, the custom was the same. The difference was that the planters would have the buggy, but we — when we could afford it — would use the horse and cart. The majority would have to walk, though. On the big day — the last Saturday in November in 1908 — I walked the mile and a half with my father-giver[12] from Freeman's Ville to All Saints Anglican Church. Lou walked with hers from the bottom of All Saints, that was about one quarter of a mile, and we met at the church. The service was quick and quiet. By the time people understood what was happening, everything done. We got a ride on a cart to the entrance of the village and walked the rest of the way home.

Affie Goodwin give me a big cake and two bottles of wine for the wedding and told me after that I would go down in history as the youngest black man in the island to get married. (When black people start to get married at an early age, it was just about the time of World War I and they start to do so because of the religion coming from the churches around that time.)

After the wedding my family start to get big. Lou had our first boy-child in 1909 and the second in 1913. But I couldn't resist temptation, so I had other children outside.

There was no end in sight for the pressure on people. Man min naked and hungry — privation for so.[13] People couldn't bear them no longer and them start to grumble here and there. The Massas wasn't at all happy over the grumbling negas. The people was deliberately staying away from work. Some of them was sent to jail for that, but they would still stay away again. People was stealing and that put massa in a passion. The magistrate jail them and they would just steal again. People min hungry and hungry make rata a-bite baking stone.[14]

---

12. Best man.
13. People were desperately poor and hungry.
14. The saying is "a starving rat will try to eat a hot stone," i.e. people were desperately hungry.

The frustration was building up. The food was rationed and the lines was long. The change of attitude went over the whole island. Then the Englishmen get smart all of a sudden and religion come in.

No longer them try to stop us from going to church. The priests and the parsons was in every home preaching the gospel to nega people. Them say we must go to church or we would be going to hell; if we would not harken to the voice of God, we would not see His face. Them give us Bible and the hymn books and told us we must be obedient to our massas for Christ was obedient to death. I think there was hardly one Englishman in this land that was not telling the nega people how good was heaven and what we must do to get there.

Although the massas' preachermen ram them religion down our throat, them never change from doing wickedness to black people. Massa work still come first, anything else — well, that was after. The nega was still working for nothing and still going to jail when he didn't show up for work. It was still jail or licks, for religion didn't have nothing to do with that. The priests and the parsons never preach that was wrong. The most they use to do was to go to the magistrate to beg off some time from the jail or some strokes if the order was the cat-o-nine, and only if they happen to know you. Mind you, although religion didn't change the misery and the hardships, nega drink it in. The doctrine take hold early.

The priests get to be very powerful, more powerful even than the planters. Anything the priests want the people to do, it was absolute certainty that the people would do it. It seem to me, if the priests and the parsons ever wanted the injustices against black people to stop, that would be bound to happen. If the priests and the parsons wanted the people to stand up against hunger and starvation, that would have happened. If them wanted even the slightest improvement in our living conditions, it would have happened. A nar two people soak in the doctrine.[15]

The people that was as old as I was or older was less convinced about the thing. I went along living my life. I had too much

15. In a very short time the people were swayed.

experience about what the church was like for me to hear them. A good many of the preachers was planters and them was wicked, wicked, wicked. I didn't have nothing to do with any church. That's not to say I don't believe in God, but when the bakkra preachers use to tell us that if we don't obey God, hell will be our portion, I knew there couldn't be a hell hotter than North Sound. No hell could be hotter than what was going on in this land against nega people.

I remember an Anglican priest that make it absolutely clear that the Anglican church wasn't built for nega people. Nega must go to church, but they must please keep out of St. George's. That priest was right. The Anglican Churches in Antigua that wasn't built before our relations reach to this land was built when we was in chains like cattle out in the pasture. They was also built far away from the plantations and even up to now some are still out of bounds to us.

It's only nowadays that the bakkra don't swap animals on Sundays after service. I remember the first time I went to Valley Church was to follow Massa Affie one Sunday to swap horse after the service. The English planters use to love to go to church on Sundays to trade. Don't let them fool you at all.[16] The god them serve was they money and nega must slave to get that money for them. The honest planter would never be afraid to tell you that his money was his god.

Priest after priest, parson after parson use to go see my mother to try and get me to go to church. She was against them all. She use to argue with them and tell a story. It goes like this: a slave that use to have to pull his owner to church was humming a hymn on his way back home one Sunday. When his massa hear him humming the tune he give him a good licking. The following Sunday the preacher went to the slave and told him he was to get out of bounds of the church because St. Barnabas wasn't for slaves and he, the preacher wouldn't like to hear that the slave get licks again for the same thing. My mother use to ask the preacher man or priest where the preacher gone, hell or heaven?

Whatever the massas want done was what the church done.

16. Don't think religion was the only reason they went to church.

Maybe there was a few exceptions, but the usual thing was for the church to protect the bakkra while we suffer and die of hunger and starvation.

Them church people use to hang on the walls of Big Church[17] and St. Peter's the names of the people that serve the church well. Nearly all of them names was of slave owners or people that didn't care nothing about negas. I bet anything that no black person name was on them walls before 1914. That was about the time that nega people start to get involved in them church.

The white priest use to put it in the head of the black churchman that he's better than other nega people and he would go on like he's better than his own poor brethren. The black fool immediately forget where he come from. I use to do anything other than to hear them priests and preachers. It was just not right for our people to listen to them.

Them preachermen get to be frantic when England was at war. The planters love Great Britain. They was in this island, but they prayers was always for the great British Empire. I always have the feeling that they would die with pleasure defending England, but them not give a damn for us.

When World War I broke out in 1914, my boss, Mass Affie went to fight. A bullet hit him in the face, but he use to tell me that he never thought of dying, that he went to fight for his country, England, and provided that his country didn't lose, he didn't care whether he dead or not.

During the war years wherever there was a group of white people, you would be right if you guess they would be talking about how was the war going. Any little gathering of planters, the topic was sure to be the war. News didn't come by so quickly back then and they was anxious to know what was happening. They use to get into the churches and pray to them God and sing songs for the Mother Country like "Rule Britannia, Britannia rule the waves' Britannia never, never shall be slaves". Another song they use to sing with all them might was "I will not cease from mental fight, Nor shall my sword sleep in my hands, Till we have built Jerusalem, In England's green and pleasant land".

7. The main Anglican Cathedral in St. John's.

The churches use to be full up with them. Some could hardly work a day, for the war was on their mind.

The nega people was in sympathy with the massas. We love the Mother Country and we wanted her to win. We use to sing another song that goes like this at the end, "And love the land that bore you, But the Empire best of all". All the people accept that. We did love the Empire best of all. We didn't stop to think how they were treating us.

During and after the war people nearly eat one another. There seem to be no end to the hunger and starvation. The priests and parsons was all keeping things quiet. More and more people start to go to church and many of them that couldn't go on Sundays would go to the open air services at nights. Any time the moonlight was up there would be two and three services in the week. And in the midst of the preaching the people all around was dying from all manner of diseases. Every week, small as our village was, somebody dead. Ever so often you would find dead bodies in the guts[18] and ponds around the place. R.S.D. use to say that them was the people that was killing themselves. That was so. Plenty people rather dead than go on suffering every day.

During — and for some time after — the war, all the imported foodstuffs was scarce. Matches and kerosene oil was even harder to come by. For weeks we couldn't light lamps at nights for lack of oil. We would use the old tinder box instead of matches, but nothing was there to use in place of oil.

Coupons was given out to collect foodstuff, but many times there was no food to collect. That was when the planters start to give land to everybody that want land to work. Almost everybody wanted it. The good thing was that the war force the people forward. Massa give himself the right of to half — more like two-thirds — of what the produce was, but to get to work the land was a great step forward for the people.

The war slowed down everything, even cricket. Gov. Heskette Bell spent a lot of time afterwards starting up cricket again. The islands use to compete for the Heskette Bell trophy, but no cricket could be played during the war years. Cricket was my

18. Ditches.

favourite sport. Even after I get married, I use to play a little cricket. The bat was made from village wood and the ball was made from cloth knit with twine.

It was around the time of the war that the churches start to christen black people picknee, but never would they do it at the same time with the white people. The rule was wedlock christen on Sundays and bastards during the week. And all the bastards was for black people. The massas knew that. Up to 1914 most of the men was just living with the women.

I remember how people in my village would always have the feeling that I should know when they were born. Probably this come from the time when I use to help them at the night schools. It get to be worse when I get to be the oldest man in the village. I made sure that my children birth get registered, for even when them start to christen nega picknee, them priests hardly record the christening in them church register, so a large portion of the people in my young days was not accounted for. Plenty of them never register one place. But my mother told us whenever she get hard enough[19] after her baby born she always go to Parham to register the baby, so all of my brothers and sisters know when them born.

A good amount of parents use to ill-treat them own picknee. It seem to me it could be one of the hand-downs from slavery. The bakkra did not care the way our people abuse them picknee.

With all the preaching that was going on, they was still burying the dead nega separate from the white people. And when the nega man began to full up the churches, the priests start to hold separate services. One hour for black and another hour for white. The bakkra also use to have special seats that nobody could sit on. No mind how the church pack, them seat belongs to massa. No nega could sit on them seats. And they was well pad-up seats, too.

By the time the war end, most of the people was looking to Gunthorpes to employ them and some of the planters was getting less and less interested in Antigua.

Following the war, life in Antigua come much harder.

19. When she was strong enough after childbirth.

Especially in the 1930's when we get hit by more hard times — some big shots call it "depression" years — and there was two hurricanes which make it real, real hard for us.

7

Field and Factory:
It Was Work Like a Bull

The war was over and the Gunthorpes sugar factory was in full swing. Man, I tell you, the small estate mill was gradually fading out and Old Betty — that's Betty's Hope — no longer was the great Betty she used to be.

Gunthorpes took the place of Betty's Hope as the biggest employer on the island. The factory was also paying higher wages to its workers than what the estates was paying theirs. That brought some friction between the planters that own the factory and those that own the estates, for the estate owners got the beliefs that they would have to pay factory rates. That never happened.

The estate workers felt that the factory workers should get more pay than the ones working in the cane fields. They also felt those in the factory was better than the field workers, for the factory ones was learning skills and having to run machines operated by steam. In quick time the factory workers learnt not only how to operate the machines but also how to repair them. Factory man really learnt fast, I can tell you. Some workers learnt how to operate the locos,[1] drive the trucks and the cars and other equipments. They also learnt how to fit pipes and weld. And it was because of the factory that the solder-man or tinsmith came on the scene. Before the tinsmith trade reach here, whenever the pans, cups, bowls, basins and so on was leaking, clay was use to patch them up, but that kind of patch hardly last at all. Sometimes you would travel the farthest distance for a bucket or can of water and even before you reach home, the clay gone and the water start to leak out so when solder and rivets took the place of clay it was a wonderful thing. Those tinsmiths use to travel from village to village and from estate to estate with them coal, coal-pot and solder iron. "Solder man in town!", that was the cry. No more would you worry that the water leak out quietly overnight. The cups, pans, basins and other things was brought out and fixed up and made whole again. The solder-man could put handle on tin cups, make saucepans, graters, food carriers and frying pans.

Gunthorpes would import most of its goods in drums and cans, an entirely different thing to what the estate owners use to do. (Their stuff came in barrels and they didn't give those barrels away when they finish with them. Instead, they used to use them to make tubs to hold water and also to feed animals out of.) But the factory give away most of the empty drums and cans. We use to make very good use of them. The ones that wasn't in so good a shape would be fixed up by the tinsmith or somebody else that have the know-how.

I think that Gunthorpes turned out to be one of the most important things for negas since slavery end. We start to develop skills, people start to see they could learn something, that life isn't just ploughing fields, digging roots, weeding grass and dropping dung. The factory also cause the planters to neglect some of the land and people start to make use of that land. And Gunthorpes brought a whole lot of people from all over the island at one place so nega people get to know each other better. That make it so the bakkra couldn't control us getting together at the factory like they could on the estates.

1. Locomotives or trains.

Some things never change, though. The planters in the fields and factory was just the same when it come to how them treat nega people. It was work like a bull.

The hours was long and when a man at work, them couldn't ask the time. Ever so often workers was losing life and limbs at that place, but nobody cared. Families didn't have a soul to turn to for help if them father or son get hurt. It was entirely different to what the work was on the estates and it cause a whole heap of sadness in the early days. When the rail line was put in, the loco use to slip off the rail quite often and that use to cause serious injury and sometimes death. Finally, some wood were brought from Barbuda to strengthen the rail and that help to prevent the accidents. Step by step things start to change for the better as the people learnt more skills and found out how to avoid getting hurt so much.

Even as Gunthorpes was swinging along, negas was making great efforts to get the bakkra land to work. They got more land to work and if you had the luck to get some, you would work like son of man to better yourself. After the nega reap the cane, the estate owner use to collect the money for it from the factory and pay the croppers what the owner decide was enough. Crop after crop them robbed us. The small farmers would get a pittance for all them labour and sometimes nothing.

Now force make water go up hill so the small farmers start to grumble, serious grumblings. Some was working the land to help out the meagre wages they were getting. Quite a good portion of people couldn't get work anywhere so they work the land because there was nothing else for them to live by. The bakkra kept on robbing the small farmer blind. In most cases you would just be working the land for the estate. You would get to feel you should have the right to collect your cane money straight from the factory. That was the main grumble.

When the factory management found out about the grumbling, in quick time they make it clear that neither the factory nor the small farmers have the right to the cane money. Factory say that the proprietors alone have that right and the factory will not pay any money whatsoever to the small farmers. It was the first time most of us ever hear the word "proprietor".

I know I didn't know the meaning of the word. Affie Goodwin told me "proprietor" was the estate owners and that I, Samuel Smith, will never live to see the factory pay the small owners unless that is what the owners want. And if the small farmers want to make trouble, they will be told to leave the land.

For the first time in my lifetime, the nega people was standing up. When the word got around people didn't get scared, it was time enough for people to really get fed up. Them get vex. The cutters at Delaps all of sudden refuse to cut cane for the price the bakkra say. Around then Sanderson cutters did the same, and the workers at North Sound refuse to work till sundown, the usual way of doing things. The bakkra was surprised for they never accustom to that kind of a thing. The people always did what massa want. Them planters got well shook up.

The crop had just started. It was early March 1918. What happen at Delaps, Sanderson's and North Sound was not the end of things. Not by a long shot. R.S.D. Goodwin and family was staying over in St. John's the Friday night of that week in order that the family could go with Gov. Merewether and his party to the Nelson's Dockyard on Saturday. I had to along to take care of the horses and things.

When the governor and them reach All Saints crossroad on the way to the dockyard, things was already happening there. There was a large gathering of people and a man was talking to them. When he realize that the governor was passing, he shout something at the tip[2] of his voice. The governor sent over one of the horse guards that was with him to go and take the man's name and address, but he didn't have him get arrested. Later that day R.S.D. said to me that trouble was just around the corner and I must, do God bless, keep out. He went on to tell me that the man speaking was one Charlie Martin of All Saints — he lived at Nevis Street in town — and that he a-shout[3] that the small farmers must demand their pay from the factory. The crowd was mostly small farmers. After the horse guard came and got Charlie's name and address, the crowd broke up.

2. Shout out loud.
3. He'd been shouting.

Meeting done. This was the first of that kind of meeting to happen in the island in my time. Except for church service, you couldn't hold any meeting in this island.[4]

From then on I was of the feeling that All Saints ought to be the seat of Council in Antigua. Not only did Charlie Martin have guts to do such a thing, the people gathered there have a lot of guts, too.

When something start to happen, it seldom stop for some time. The next week — after the meeting of All Saints — trouble broke out at Palmer Jelly, where the cutters refuse to cut the fields unless they were burnt first. From what R.S.D. said, the planters decide that they were going to make example of some of them cutters and summon the ringleaders before the magistrate when the fields at Palmer Jelly catch ablaze. Not long after that, fire broke out at Villa Estate and the cane fields at Gambles was also set on fire.

At Gambles the planters was panicking and the police went in and told people in the name of the King to go and help put out the fire. At the same time the police got a tip off that one George Weston of the point was the man that lit the fields at Palmer Jelly. The police, they went to take George away for questioning, but the people at the Point told them that George knows nothing about the fire, so he isn't going anywhere with any police.

When the police try to arrest George Weston the people then and there turn mad. The police have to run from them bottles and stones and try to get reinforcements. (The police force at the time was numbering about twenty to twenty-five and they use to be the police for the Leeward Islands and Dominica, part of the Leewards back then.) When they come back with the reinforcement a riot broke out and they couldn't make a hand[5] of the Point people. The massas call out the militia and when they come the riot really spread. No longer was it riot between the Point people and the police, now it was between nega and white. The militia and the defence force — except for a few high-

4. No political meetings for blacks were permitted.
5. The police couldn't control events at the Point.

coloured police — was all white.

The councillors got called to government house for an emergency meeting about the riot. In those days, it was the horse guards that use to carry government messages to the planters and them sure got the message in quick time, for them horses could move fast. By now it was Saturday, a day when people from all over the island was normally in St. John's. It was also the usual thing in those days for the hucksters to be at the market on the Friday evening or very early on the Saturday morning. The big shots, too, would always be doing some business in town on a Friday and they would tell their people about the happenings. On that Saturday there were crowds of people all over the place, mostly in front of and around the police headquarters, in Big Church yard, and on East Street where the governor was living. If you didn't have a stick, you had a stone or something else. People was determined that George Weston will not be arrested.

The planters start gathering at government house about midday. By then, the crowd — particularly around government house — was getting to be bigger and bigger. People wanted to know what was going on inside, what would happen. About two o'clock the meeting done and the planters start to get out of town.

R.S.D. Goodwin told his people to get inside, for the offenders was going to be arrested and anybody that resist will get shot. I knew what was the result of the meeting before word go to the angry crowd outside. Even so, the bakkra waste very little time to let people know what was the decision. The magistrate court — it was on East Street — was opened up and the officer sounded the drums and told everybody to draw near and hear. People like ticks draw near. Them drums roll again and magistrate Solomon Reed read the Riot Act. The way I was told, the militia was suppose to fire warning shots and tell the crowd to clear out, but that never happen.

Not one warning shot was there. Just the regular shots. The people start to run for them lives. In quick time the streets was clear. Not a man around, except for the ones that couldn't move. Some people got shot in their legs, some in the arms and back.

Two or three got their arms shot off. R.S.D. told me he was quite sure that people have learnt their lessons.

The policemen then went for George Weston and a whole lot of other people. They arrest these men and charge them with all sorts of things. Some of the cutters that refuse to work the cane fields before the fields got burnt was also arrested. Charlie Martin — the man that had the meeting at All Saints — got word that the police was looking for him. He took a schooner and left the island. In those days, you don't have to have passports or nothing like that to travel and there was no restriction to enter any of the islands. They never catch Charlie Martin. Some others got away too.

The Sunday after the riot the priest at St. Peter's told the people in the church that any of them that cause that kind of trouble must not come to him to beg for them. The people the planters said was behind the whole thing got properly dealt with. I remember that George Weston got seven years hard labour. Others got four and some got up to six years hard labour. The home of the negas was still prison for the least thing. Now them riot, them better expect anything, the planters say. The planters make it clear that they will deal hard with any and all workers that refuse to work. I think it was after the riot that the people of Antigua got to be afraid of guns. Everything went still. Small farmers decide to make out, no more public grumbling from them. Them just grunt and bear it. No more refusal to work from anybody — at least that I know of — for quite a while. R.S.D. was of the belief that once and for all the people learnt their lesson and will never behave that way again. I thought that what R.S.D. said — remember I knew the man a long time — was the view of the governor and all the other bakkra.

Not a single soul — worker or farmer — got a farthing more on the pay during the last three years of Gov. Merewether. Not one copper more. That was in spite from the riot. From what I know, the governor was the first after slavery to use guns on the people. He did exactly what the planters wanted, he push poor people further back. During his last days as the governor, you use to see a whole lot more beggars in Antigua and plenty people didn't have place to lay their heads at nights.

The small farmers went on working the land under some very rough conditions. At the same time, the donkey start to be the most treasured animal for the farmer. It's strong and easy to care for. The donkey use to carry the water to the villages from any part of the island. It was the donkey that took us to the doctor. The poor people couldn't buy horses and buggies, neither a horse and cart. The donkey couldn't carry a house, but I think that's about the only thing it didn't carry for us.

In 1921, Gov. Fiennes took the place of Gov. Mereweather. The worst governor I ever see was replaced by the best governor in my lifetime. When I say best, I mean the one I think did the most good to the island generally.

Within the same year, my wife had her fifth and last child for me. By then I had thirty-five children alive. That number isn't too much because I start to make children in 1894, when I was seventeen, and to have two a year would be normal.

I got to know Gov. Fiennes. He was a melle man.[6] He love nega business and he got to know what was happening in the island. I think he very well understood the feelings of the negas. He took pride in his work and he wanted that his term of office would mean something to the people.[7] For me, he was entirely different to all the governors that reach the island before and I believe he will remain the best ever.

By this time I was so tied to work that my family was getting to be neglected somewhat. Besides doing almost everything on the estate, the Goodwins use to go on like I was a professional animal doctor and they wouldn't trust anybody else but me to look after their animals. I had to make sure all the animals was washed and attended to every week. It didn't matter what else I had to do, I had to make sure that the sick ones was tended till them get better. I worked like son of man[8] without even thinking that I was neglecting my family.

I went on working and the governor set about solving the water problem. The washing of the land when it rained use to

---

6. The governor was very well informed about other people's business.
7. The governor wanted to be favourably remembered by the public.
8. Work extremely hard.

cause land to get hard quick. That hampers the growth of the sugar cane and the vegetation generally in the land and also makes the water holes go shallow. Fisher Pond — we use to call it Body Pond — in the Swetes Village area was the main water supply. The governor had the pond dug out much deeper and bigger, some four or five times its original size. He also told the planters to dig guts[9] in every water course and to plant grass around the various water courses to prevent the land from washing out and filling up the guts quickly with mud. The governor also introduced contouring the hillside.

The planters did what he said and built guts in water courses where there was none and they dig wells. At the time there was the General Spring at the North Sound area. Guts, ponds and wells was all over the land for the first time and the water situation was not too bad. Now the main problem was how to get the water to the villages.

I remember when the tax come in for the first time. The governor put in a horse and cart tax. In fact, me think that every drawn carriage was taxed. All the planters was outraged at the tax. At the time Bendals Well — they use to call it Fiennes Well — was being built to strengthen the water supply. The governor had a big ceremony for the opening of the well with the councillors and the other planters present. I remember there was a Mr. Wilson there and he was dead against that tax. He was a teacher and later was the editor of the Magnet newspaper. Gov. Fiennes liked music so a band was also there. At the ceremony the governor talked about how the tax was to build the well and that it wouldn't apply after the opening ceremony. Then even the people that was against the tax start to compliment and praise the governor. Soon after, he started running pipe to the villages so that people could get pipe water and he got some concrete tanks built. We use to call them Fiennes' tanks.

A while later the governor said he was going to make St. John's into a tourist city. He start up by building the jetty down on High Street and another one at Fort James. He fixed up the house at the fort, clean up the whole place and made it attractive,

9. Ditches.

put in two bathrooms, and use to hire the house to anybody that wanted to spend time there. He also clean up Goat Hill, the Lighthouse and other old places on the island. He was living in Canada for some time and he started to invite the Canadians to visit Antigua. Whenever the visitors reach the island, he was sure to be there to meet them.

During the same time, when he was making St. John's into a tourist city, the governor start a programme of planting trees for food, medicine and shelter. The people catch the fever and start to plant, too. I remember when he and Lady Fiennes planted the first willow trees at the hospital, the workers planted the rest. In fact, I think that Gov. Fiennes encourage people to plant willow trees because he have the belief that the willows attract rain.

The health situation also improved under the governor. For one thing, one Sunday morning he round up all the bakers that was sleeping in the various bread shops and took them down to the police station himself. No charges was brought against them, though. What the governor did was that he order all bakers in town[10] and food handlers to a medical pass before they could handle food again. That order was rough, for back then people was sick. A whole lot of them had sores. (Up to that time, we didn't know anything about diseases or sugar. There was plenty sores that wouldn't heal and some of them could have been caused by the sugar diabetes.) There was a woman from St. John's by the name of Miss Jenkins. She use to make some clean gone cakes.[11] She sure had the rush.[12] Christmas couldn't pass and me no buy Miss Jenkins cakes, but she had a licking sore-foot. When the governor gave the order she knew that she couldn't get a health pass with that sore-foot. She couldn't go on making the cakes without the pass so she went to country pond and drowned herself.

Gov. Fiennes was a spree man.[13] He liked his dancing, so he start to have dances and parties for the government workers.

10. St. John's.
11. A type of cake.
12. People liked her cakes very much.
13. One who likes dancing and parties and other fun.

Policemen and nurses use to have regular dances and other kinds of entertainment. It was the common thing for Gov. Fiennes and his wife always to occupy the dance floor alone for quite a while at a party. There use to be a dance called the heel and toe dance, or the cuffie dung dance. Nobody could do that dance better than the governor and his wife. He was a man to dance with anybody and talk to anybody anywhere, the first governor to talk like arwe[14] sometimes. The bakkra got to be unhappy with him for that. He was also very strict with the bringing up of children, they must be in school, he said.

Although the governor did a lot of things to improve the island, the wages was still very low. Most negas would find it hard to buy dinner, and sometimes you didn't know where the next meal was coming from. The year 1924 made six straight years that the workers in the fields and the factories went without a pay raise. Probably it was longer but I am only counting the years after the riot. In that same year — 1924 — the cutters refuse to work for the money they was getting. This time there was no big quarrel or threat of being taken before the magistrate. Gov. Fiennes settle the problem by asking the planters to give everybody a raise. They gave it. What the planters gave was a pittance, but better little bit than nothing at all. I think that if we had somebody to speak for us in those days, we could have made some progress under Gov. Fiennes.

The island was also hit by two hurricanes in 1924. Hurricanes wasn't named like today and back then we never knew when they were coming. Death and damage was always heavy when they hit us. Them storms sure brought a lot of rain. Country Pond was burst in two and Tanner Street — that was the genuine outlet to the sea — but the force of the water cut Nevis Street in two halves and the water came pouring through. In them days, there was no black oil roads. The material that was on the road would wash away quick by the force of that kind of water. You could call Fiennes "the Hurricane Governor" because in 1928, before his term of office end, another hurricane hit the island.

I still remember very well the governor that was in office just

14. Like us, like Antiguans.

before Fiennes — Mereweather — and how when he finish here there was a good portion of poor people without a job and a home. But Gov. Fiennes felt that one of his last tasks to the island was to do something about that. He decided to build a home for the real poor, sick and shelterless people. The bakkra get angry over that and report him to the Colonial Office. The governor answer back that if he was not getting the money from England to build the poor house, then he would get it from the people. The money must be found somewhere, he say. He had his way and built the poor house — the Fiennes Institute — just on the eastern side of the hospital.

Right away there was too many people wanting to be there. The governor looked at a plan to cut the number of people there. Then he organized a dance and he and his wife danced with them. At the end of the dance, everybody that danced well was told to leave and find work to do. That trick was the melle[15] around town for a long time. The governor went one more step when he built a church for them, for priest hardly ever had dealings with poor house people back then. In fact, I would be glad to know if any big time preacherman has been there up to now.

During the time of Gov. Fiennes, bus service — it was privately owned — came to Antigua for the first time. It had the name Lady Fiennes and was used mainly to carry people to places like Fort James and Goat Hill. Around the same time the Gunthorpes factory was expanding. There was new machinery installed and the factory was able to grind more canes in a shorter time. Some estate owners introduced the steam plough, but it didn't work like them expected. The planters said it was slow and expensive.

During the same time the Portuguese businessmen built shops in some villages and the Lebanese people was selling cloth, walking from door to door with their bundles under the arms, on the arms or on their heads to sell them goods.

Time always have its way. Sometime in 1929, the term of Gov. Eustace Fiennes, the ordinary melle man, was up. Except

15. What he did was the talk of the town for a long time.

for the planters, people everywhere was sad. Gov. St. Johnson — that man was a bad-minded man — took his place. St. Johnson tried to mash up everything he meet ya.[16] He left Fort James and Goat Hill to go to ruin, never spent a copper to keep them clean all the years he was here. Neither did he maintain the jetty on High Street. And he wasn't too happy over building the homes for the poor. A few yards away from the poor house, he build some houses and name them St. Johnson's Village. Me think he put them up because he wanted to rival Gov. Fiennes or look a name himself.[17]

Sometime after St. Johnson's Village was built — in 1931 or around there — we had some very exciting times. Airplane land in St. John's harbour for the first time. The crop was in full swing and the day was a Sunday. I remember it very well, how at the sound of the plane everybody scamper, people run for them life — we all thought it was Judgement Day — man even run out of the churches to hide. I think that the church was the best place for judgement to meet people.

Under Gov. St. Johnson there was no work. Everything crash. People min a dead for hungry.[18] Nineteen thirty-four came, the one hundredth anniversary of the end of slavery. It should have been a time for celebration, a time for joy, but there was nothing to jump for. Most of the people were still living in misery on the estates and one hundred years after slavery the living conditions on the estates was no better than during slavery time. The bakkra neglect our people except when they go to jail. When that happen, the bakkra always make sure them wasn't neglected by the full weight of the law.

Some other notable events took place around the same time. A black man, S.L. Athill, got to be a magistrate and a member of the Council. In 1934, some Portuguese built a rum distillery down at Rat Island. Before the still was built people all over use to make them own rum from cane juice or molasses mixed with water and yeast. Next you would let it ferment and then put it to

16. He ruined things.
17. Wanted to be famous.
18. People died from starvation.

boil. Then you would put it in demi-john and the demi-john would then be put under the earth. There under the earth the rum would come to its right flavour. If there was no demi-john, you would find something else to use. We call the rum Speak Easy. Around the same time that the still was set up, the planters brought a new plough call the gyrotiller. That plough cause a lot of excitement amongst sugar workers for it could plough the land and bank it at the same time. Although the gyrotiller worked well in some of the places, people say it usually plough the land too deep. The machine was great, but it didn't replace the old plough. And by that time, I had a total of forty-three children. Some carry my title[19] but quite a lot of them did not. I was at the time still doing everything on the estate, labouring like the son of man. My father died in 1935. I have not seen anybody that could make better baskets than that man.

I think it was soon after the coming of the gyrotiller plough that Gov. St. Johnson left the land. Most of us was glad to see him go back home. The next governor was Gov. Gordon Lethem and he also didn't care about the growing misery and starvation amongst the people. He care more for horse racing. Under him, horse racing got to be a national sport and people from all over the island was always sure to be at the races.

19. Some went by the name Smith.

8

Organizing:
Force Makes Water
Go Up Hill

While the governor and the big shots were betting on the horses and having themselves a good time, the people was walking from pillar to post — just can't get work. People use to walk from Freeman's Ville to York's Estate — about twelve miles — to work for one shilling a day. I think that work was harder to get at that time than any other time in my life.

Most of the plantation mills was fading out and — except for the Bendal's factory that closed in 1940 or so — I don't remember seeing any of the estate's mills operating at that time. That was the cause for so many jobless people.

Of course, the Gunthorpes factory was doing well. It was doing what it was built to do: grind all the canes. The sugar factory at that time was managed by one of the most powerful man in the island, one L.I. Henzel. A powerful little man. And ruthless. If Henzel speaks, the workers heareth. Henzel act, the workers suffereth. Again and again he use to get rid of workers only for the look of their faces.

When Henzel happen to pass through Gunthorpes, every man

there would have to stand up straight like arrows or home them gone.[1] Sometimes when workers watch him pass by, he fire them. If they don't watch him, he still fire them. But of all the wicked things he did to workers, I think that what happen in the turkey incident was among the worst, for it hurt over five hundred workers at one stroke.

What happen was that where Henzel was living at Painters Estate he lost a turkey. Painters was not too far from the Factory. Just about one quarter of a mile, if so much. Henzel was of the belief that some worker stole the turkey, and that person had to be a factory worker. He couldn't say who did it, but he took six pence from the pay of each worker to make up the loss. So each worker paid for the turkey. The value of that turkey was more than any house and land in them days.

Not very long after, the turkey show up with a brood of chicks. Henzel show a great deal of happiness when he tells the workers about that, but I hardly get the feeling that he was of the belief that he done something wrong. He never give back the money. None of them could drunk say anything.[2]

Some people that worked in the small gang didn't take home any pay that week because them wasn't even getting six pence a week.

Around the time of the turkey happening, news were reaching Antigua of disturbances in the other islands, something that the Antigua planters take very seriously. A whole lot of them gather at the great house at Collin's to talk about the riots in the other islands. At that meeting the bakkra pledge to do everything to keep that kind of thing from reaching Antigua. Some time later news reach the island that the group of Englishmen that was going around the islands to settle the problems was coming to Antigua. (The thing is, all kinds of problems start up among the planters and the people in the other islands.) Towards the end of 1938 they reach here.

The planters had themselves several meetings about the situation before and after the group got to Antigua. Quite a few

1. Workers had to stand at attention or be fired.
2. Even drunk they dared not complain.

of them meetings was at the great house.

Early in 1939, a representative of the group, a man by the name of Sir Walter Citrine, told the people in St. John's that they should have a union to represent them. It then appear like the usual councillor's feast at the great house that year was bigger than usual.

Some days after the feast, Affie Goodwin drop off some words to me. He said, like this, "So you all going to have union? If people want union, we will do nothing to stop it." I conclude to myself then and there that probably was the decision of the planters.

Some weeks after Affie Goodwin dropped the words to me, a group of men came to where I was working at Duers Estate. They told us that the best thing that can help us out of the hard times was a union and that we must get together. The following week another group come. This group have sticks with them and they approach the different gangs. I think I see them right now. They ask you, "You get together yet?" If the answer was "no" you would get licks. It was like this, "You get together?" Whap! "You get together?" Whap! Licks like peas. They would go from estate to estate doing the same thing. There was sure no joke with this getting together in them days.

At the same time, a meeting was held at Osbourne pasture where Leonard Benjamin,[3] Luther George[4] and others spoke. After that meeting the workers, them strike for almost everything. We were in a fighting mood. Sometime during the crop of 1940 there was another meeting held at the same spot. The speakers told us that Gov. Lethem pass the law to allow us to form the union, and if we strike till the canes rotten in the fields, nobody could take us to court like before when you could get jail for missing work just once.

The people was anxious to get on with the union, but the planters, they felt that the union couldn't last for too long. That was them view again and again. They was saying that nobody in the island have any idea of how to run the union, that the people

3. Prominent early AT & LU activist.
4. Prominent early AT & LU activist.

would fight amongst themselves and mash it up. Me too was also fearful that the people would do just that because some of our people have always had a weakness over the years to carry news on each other to the bakkra and news carrying mash up anything.

By the time the union start to form, a good portion of black people was high up in the church. There was quite a few local preachers that start to take a lead in the union. At the same time, there was also some well-to-do nega people that had the feeling that they was white. Some of them was operating business in the island. Them well-to-do pretend not to know what was happening. Most of them was against the union. That's the way them was at the time.

A short, brown-skinned man by the name of Reginald Stevens was the union's first president. I knew him long before he ever dreamt of becoming president of such a thing called union. Stevens was accustom to deal with planters so I was not surprised when he got to be the union's first president. He was a big man in the Odd Fellows Lodge and he had been to Duers a few time to beg Affie Goodwin for some of his members when they was having problems. I was of the belief that Stevens was doing the same thing some place else.

The Antigua Trades and Labour Union was hardly born when World War II breaks out and, of course, a war England was mixed up in was sure to slow up the growth of the union. In those days, though the people was covered from head to foot in misery, England come first to all of us. She was the Mother Country, but even if we think different, the bakkra would never let the union to interfere with the war efforts. But the leaders worked hard anyway and set up union committees in every village, in every part of the land. The first chairman of the committee of Freeman's Ville, where I lived, was a Methodist preacher by the name of Thadeous James.

By the end of 1941, Gov. Jardine took the place of Gov. Lethem. World War II was raging hot. There was talk that the Germans was coming to attack the islands. The English government hired Miller's Estate to the United States to build a military base to boot up the local forces on the island. The

Camacho family — one of the richest on the island — was the owners of Miller's and that family wept bitter tears, for they didn't want to give up Miller's Buff with its most beautiful rose garden. I think it was about then that Gov. Jardine lost his wife. She was the first governor's wife to be buried at Number Ten.

Jardine left and Governor Freeston took over. Freeston use to remind me of Gov. Fiennes in at least one respect — he use to stop and talk to anybody.

The war was occupying the mind of everybody, but in quick time the union made three great steps ahead. It get a good wage increase and was improving conditions of work for the workers at Gunthorpes. It also got the portion of land reduced that a woman would have to work for a farming. The woman that worked farming usually had to take a week and a half or so before them work was complete and that was for only eightpence a farming. That period would be longer when the rain come plenty. Besides getting the portion of field cut back for the women, the union made the planters to finish with the half-land farming. Now that was a great thing for small farmers. Stevens to them was Moses. It was unbelievable what the union got done. The good news spread like wildfire, but the union was shackle and couldn't do the things that would have made it get even more success.

Not very long after, the president, St. Clair Reginald Stevens, was remove from office. Vere Bird took his place. I couldn't understand why the union change its president just when it was making some impossible breakthroughs. That change sure cause stir for awhile. I was wondering if the planters' hope that the union was going to destroy itself was coming to pass.

At a meeting at Burke's pasture, the new president and his people told why the conference move Stevens. They said at the meeting that Stevens could have got more for the Gunthorpes workers, but he wasn't keen to do that and that he wasn't as honest as he look. Hearing this, them say the conference had to drop the ball.[5]

I think that business about the honesty was just a lie to poison

5. That he would have to be replaced.

the minds against Stevens. Me remember that it was earlier that same year, when the same people say Stevens was great for what he was doing. It was that same year that the same people told us at a meeting at the same spot that it was a God-send that Stevens was the president because he was paying the union's organizers out of his own pocket. The same people said that if it wasn't for Stevens, the union could never be organized that quick because there was no money. Stevens, they told us back then, was footing the union's bills. (It is true that Stevens could never be a pauper. Council wasn't for poor people and he was one of the few people that have enough money to run for Council.) I just don't know for other people, but I know for myself that it was Stevens that give the union a flying start and a solid foundation in the early days. And I believe that one of these days we might find out exactly what happen to my good friend Stevens.

The union was changing. So too was the planters. The old planters that hold the stage for a long time was coming off the scene. L.I. Henzel get sick and lose his voice. Man, the powerful Henzel couldn't say a word. Not a word. All he have to say have to be written down on a piece of paper. The Camacho brothers was also fading out and R.S.D. reach his seventieth birthday and decide to take a back seat on things. A new powerful man, Alexander Moody Stuart, got to be the leader and spokesman of the planters.

Around the same time, Gov. Freeston decide to give permission to some rich Americans to build some houses east of Freetown and to put in the Mill Reef Club. The union's big man immediately protest to the governor against that Mill Reef Club. He said that the club was going to be a South Africa or a Alabama where black people get treated worse than dogs. He ask the governor not to allow the club. The governor didn't even look at him. You see, the construction work at the American military bases was petering out and the members of the union was glad to get a bite at Mill Reef. The new leaders of the Antigua Trade and Labour Union start to realize the value of the club and them stop attacking it.

The war was still going on. There was some improvements in

the land, but the laws that treat nega people like the beasts of the fields was still going strong and the planters never miss any opportunity to punish nega people.

Just about that time the sugar syndicate start to form, Blakes Estate was privately owned and it was paying a little more money than the other estates — a woman, one Lolita Emmanuel of Bethesda, left working at Maurice Looby and went to Blakes to work. Up to that time, nobody could leave from one estate to another to work without permission. The bakkra of Maurice Looby took Lolita to the magistrate for going to Blakes to work. Magistrate Athill gave her six days hard labour.

Time always move on. The war was over. Vere Bird was in the place of Stevens on the Council and the Antigua Trade and Labour Union got into politics in 1946. The controls on the union because of the war was over and the people was ready to do anything and everything to make life come better.

But the planters have all confidence in Alexander Moody Stuart. Them determine to fight against anything and everything that look like it is in the favour of the people.

By then age was creeping up on me. I was the only person that was around Duers for so long. A tense fight was coming between the planters — led by Alexander Moody Stuart — and the Antigua Trade and Labour Union. By 1947, I finish fifty non-stop years at Duer's and I was never sick, neither absent from work for a day in my life. During that same year I reach my seventieth birthday and Gov. Baldwin came to take the place of Gov. Freeston.

I think it was around that same time that the cutters make a demand to change the way of payment from the ton to the line.[6] The cutters said them couldn't count them money. Them want to know how the planters arrive at how much them work for. The cutters and the union was of the belief that cutting canes per line would let everybody know how much them work for everyday. In the end there was a strike over the thing. While the strike was on, a man by the name of Skeeple went all over the

6. Line payment was made according to a certain number of feet of canes.

island ringing a bell and calling out the death of the ton. The union won the battle. Ton was stiff dead. That strike last for some nine weeks — the longest strike ever to be up to that time.[7]

Things was starting to look up. Workers was demanding and getting respect from the planters. Gov. Baldwin was giving some backing to the demands of the union. The planters carry news on him to the Colonial Office and he was called back to England. Most of the people was unhappy that Baldwin was force to leave. There was even a song that went, "Earl Baldwin must come back, In his suit of black." He did come back and he got a great welcome back to the land. But much to the surprise of everybody, Baldwin resign some months later.

Baldwin left in 1950 and the island was hit by two hurricanes that same year. The second hurricane knocked down almost all the wattle and daub houses. A lot of people was still living on the estates at the time. The planters wanted them off because they said the people didn't have to pay house rent or have to meet bank.[8] The times was already changed and the planters couldn't handle the workers like they use to in the old days. They also didn't feel too happy that people was refusing to work the Monday after the public holidays. In fact, we use to call the Tuesday after a public holiday Blue Tuesday. The Antigua Trade and Labour Union was in full swing and because of the hurricanes it ask the government for better houses for the people. It got the houses so them hurricanes prove to be a blessing in disguise.

During 1950 R.S.D. Goodwin dead. He was put to rest at the foot of the garden of the Great House. I think he was the last of the planters to be buried at home. Like John Ireland[9] — one of the best union officers I ever knew and somebody that use to have many, many fights with R.S.D. said at a public meeting — when God call, arwe have to go. The mighty R.S.D. is dead. Affie Goodwin too, was dead. He died two years or so before in Canada and Duers was taken over by the sugar syndicate.

---

7. The 1940 strike had lasted seven weeks.
8. Bank loans to pay off.
9. Prominent early AT & LU activist.

In 1951, it was strike from the word go. Like I tell you, force make water go up hill. The president of the AT & LU declared that not a blade of cane would get cut till the price got settled. The strike went on for several weeks. After it was over the workers decide for the first time to celebrate May Day. When the people went back to work on the next day the planters drove them off the estates and closed down the reaping. The planter boss, Alexander Moody Stuart, decide not to recognize the unions anymore. That was the first time that happen since 1939. He told Levi Joseph[10], John Ireland and Malcolm Daniel, officers of the AT & LU not to go on the estates. That wasn't all. Then he made it known all around that nobody was going to be allowed on any land belonging to the syndicate. He was going to be the one to say where the people should walk.

At the same time, the union wanted them lands to be taken away from the syndicate. The union was of the belief that the government should own the land so that the small farmers couldn't be driven off at any time. The union hit back by calling a general strike. It was head on clash between the planters and the union. War between Moody Stuart and the union. Antigua hot like fire. The people was behind the union. Moody Stuart said he was going to starve out the people. The fight was on. There were violence here and there. Some buildings in St. John's was set ablaze. Gov. Blackburn got afraid the thing would get out of hand and he called in the British fleet from Jamaica.

The governor got the union and the planters to agree to an inquiry, the Malone Inquiry. If memory serve me right, a man by the name of Richard Hart from Jamaica was speaking for the union at the inquiry and Lawyer Christian was representing for the planters.

The workers didn't let Moody Stuart starve them out. The end was victory for the union, but quite a few of the strong members suffer the consequences of Magistrate Athill. Men from Bethesda, All Saints, Sea View Farm and Parham all did time in jail.

In my mind, 1951 got to be the best year since the end of

10. Prominent early AT & LU activist.

slavery. What happen that year set the stage for what was going to come. The union was also doing other serious business. It was advancing in politics. By then the Council had nominated members — planters — and elected members — from the union. The nominated members outnumbered the elected ones by three. The union got the Council to add three more seats to the elected side and got the number even. That was also when the rule was changed so that you could vote at age twenty-one, whether you could read and write or not. When the Council hold the elections in 1951 and the union got all the elected seats, the two sides really start to square up.

Negas was scoring great gains. The union winning on all sides in 1951 gave a very clear sign that it was just a matter of time before massa have to go back home to England.

Nineteen fifty-one was also the year that people start to get some compensation for the first time when they would get damage or killed on the job. I'm pretty sure that 1951 was also the first time plenty people even hear the word compensation.

All this time the union was having its own problems. By then there was a change in the General Secretary four times and quite a number of people that help to organize it was out. My good friend Ashley Kirwan was out, so too was Leonard Benjamin — former Vice-president of the AT & LU and member of Council. Hugh Pratt — he was once the AT & LU Treasurer and also a member of Council — was gone. I am of the belief that Pratt got forced out because he didn't vote the way the president wanted him to in some Council matter. Pratt later said it was a slip of the pen. Samuel James — he was the union's third General Secretary — was out and so was Kem Roberts — one of the most militant men I ever knew. Roberts lost his job at the firm of Joseph Dew & Sons because he was so strong for the union. Roberts was the first Vice-president and was the union officer that organize the powerful waterfront workers. He was a forceful speaker for the union and doing everything to defend the workers. The people use to call him "Bustamante".[11]

11. A comparison to the Jamaican trade union leader and statesman, Bustamante, who founded an industrial union in Jamaica in 1938 and, in 1943, founded the Jamaica

There was a strong rumour going around that Roberts could get to be the president of the union and so the president make sure that never happen. Maybe the ousting of Luther George, another founding father of the union, was the most painful thing to see. When George was kicked out he was on a hospital bed in Jamaica. The people that was out of the union was called boo-boos and the union big shots told the people that the boo-boos was traitors, so the people harass them.

While all this was going on, any new ideas or programmes that come from anybody or any group of persons that wasn't a union big shot was looked down on. If it wasn't the president's idea, it wasn't any good.

The homes, families and gardens festival — it use to be a week long festival — that was set up by Gov. Blackburn was set aside. (That programme use to help the people keep themselves clean, let them know how to keep better homes, taught the people how to keep out of trouble and how to use the little you have in the best possible way. The best kept gardens and villages use to get prizes.) The president and his people in the union got people to boycott the festival so it fade out after a while. They even run picnics at Fry's Bay to boycott the horse races that was on almost every public holiday.

The horse races fade out, too. And New Year's Day also use to be the big thing here, but the union president told the people not to play any mass[12] to amuse the white people. The president also discourage our people from supporting the formation of credit unions. It was a general belief that the union could not take over the credit unions. Therefore members were asked to stay clear of credit unions.

Labour Party (JLP). At the time of the founding of the JLP, Jamaica was still a British colony, but the JLP won the elections and Bustamante became Chief Minister. Upon Independence in 1962 he became Jamaica's first Prime Minister.
12. Don't perform masquerade to amuse the whites.

9

The Final Years:
I Am Here to Watch and See Till the Lord Takes Me

The union kept on fighting for the people in every direction and the conditions of life start to get better.

In 1954 my mother died at age ninety-eight. I was seventy-seven and on her death I got to be the oldest person in the village. By then I was working between Duers and Delaps. The Goodwins was all gone. Now I was working for the sugar syndicate and Mr. DeSouza was my new boss. He put in for my long service pay and he also raised my Christmas bonus. By that time there was some drastic changes in the fields and the Gunthorpes factory.

The cattle plough was no more. Instead machines was being used to pull the canes and plough the fields. The factory also had changed from steam to electricity and there was quite a large number of bikes, motor bikes, cars and other such things in the country. Life move faster nowadays.

In 1956, I lost one of my dear sons, Harold. He was a Methodist local preacher and a well-known man in the union. In 1957 the heads of the Antigua Trades and Labour Union — they was really the leaders of the land — introduce the Carnival on the same date that slavery was put to its end. Now I think to do that was craziness. The coming generations will not remember that August 1 was the Emancipation Day and if it is one date that black people should remember it is that first day of August from 1834. That day should stand clear of all celebrations. It should be like the American or Haiti independence day — not to be forgotten.

It was in 1957, also, that Gov. Blackburn finish as governor. I remember him as the man who held the power of governor during the time when negas in this land was making the biggest strides ahead. One Gov. Williams took his place. I never heard that man, neither have I ever seen him, so I can't tell you what he did in his time.

By then the union leaders was in the planters' place and at the same time they was running the union. The Colonial Secretary use to tell them that they shouldn't run the union and be the government leaders at the same time. But at a public meeting at Freeman's Ville, the union leaders make it known to everybody and anybody that the Colonial Office didn't have the right to tell them what they can do.

Alexander Moody Stuart — the big shot planter — went back to England and his son George took over the estates and the factory. Disgruntlement were in the union and amongst the workers generally. It appear like the union was losing its drive. The leaders was in an embarrassing position. Myself, too, was in conflict with some of my family. I was of the view that the leaders of the union shouldn't be planters and union leaders at the same time, that the union should get somebody else to keep up the fight for the workers. Some of my people didn't think so. They got to feel that I was against the union, but that wasn't the case at all.

During the last years of my working life the planters was finding it harder and harder to get the young generations to work in the fields. Sugar is bull work — slavery. The young people do not know what name bull work.[1] Them definitely

---

1. Young Antiguans don't know what hard physical work is.

scorn field work. What made the thing worse was that the AT &
LU was telling the people that them mustn't have nothing to do
with hoe and fork. Them must throw down them hoe. Hoe dead,
them say.

Sugar was on the fade out and the hotels was just starting to
come in. The small farmers was starting to have some difficulty
to reap the crop and the people wasn't helping the parents in the
cane fields anymore. The lift that we use so much to help each
other over the years was fading out. The new generation hate
even the name sugar.

In 1962, I finally bow to the wish of my people and I decide to
retire. My last job was to tuff trench to allow the trailers to pass
by freely. The last two men that I work with was Allan Forde
and Rupert James, both was tractor drivers. They use to praise
me for how I use to work. It's a fact that I use to work better than
the young people. Hardly anybody would believe that I was
eighty-five years old. And of the eighty-five years that I live up to
then, I worked seventy-two and was never sick or late for a day.
Not once. Nobody that start working with me was around by
that time. Even people that start to work years after me was all
gone. Some time before I quit working, R.S.D. said to me that as
far as he could check, there was nobody that worked so long as
me and nobody else that work that amount of time without ever
being sick or absent — I was a superman. But I wasn't superman
and neither was I special. Almighty God was with me. I obeyed
my mother. And I was lucky, too.

When I start dropping dung back at North Sound, my mother
lament that strain never get better quick. She told me that I must
only put in the dung basket what I could lift up by myself.
Nobody must help me with the load for if that happen, then the
load is too much for me to carry. She told me also to close my
legs together when I lift up my load. She said that providing I
keep my legs together I would probably not lift more than was
good for me. She was very particular about that because a good
portion of the men back then use to get big seed.[2] The main
reason was that them strain off themselves by lifting too much

2. Hydrocele.

weight or plucking off too much mould when forking the bakkra land. Most of the forkmen back then also use to have big seed.

There was lots of men that was very strong and them use to like to show off how strong they were. Now those men hardly last too long. A man may be very strong, but flesh and blood have limit. I always remember that. Whenever we was pulling cart and I felt that the load was heavy, I wasn't afraid to take out some. I believe it's always better to make a dozen light trips than to make one big heavy one.

My mother also always use to say that when you are walking you must push your legs forward and keep your back up so you won't need a walkingstick before you really have to have one. I followed all she said and at ninety-one years I wanted no stick. I always take a little exercise just to keep my heart, neck or whatever in order. Some people is of the belief that exercise is just for the young people, but exercise is for living beings. The young and the old.

Not just my mother, but almost all my old people use to say that we must keep inside our bodies clean. They say the waste matters must come out. My mother, she was of the feeling that all the diseases come because of waste matter in the body. Have at least two bowel actions a day. We use to use aloes, salt-purge, senna, magnesia to keep the bowel active in the old days. Nowadays, there is also the Dr. Chase pills and so on.

To keep the system free of waste, eat greens of all kinds. Cassie, paw-paw, spinach, peas and things of that kind. Mix them with anything you have to eat. Too much salt is always bad. Remember that. The strong animals don't use salts. Don't use vinegar, it can keep the blood from flowing properly. We use to keep the bladder clean by using young coconut water, green bush water or inflammation bush water. When waste is out of the body, the organs inside have less work to do and they will last longer, I believe. When inside of you is clean, it's impossible to get big belly.[3] People love when them have big bellies but they don't know how them could be sick. That big belly means plenty waste in them body.

3. Bloated.

I didn't always get the good food to eat. In fact, maybe I was eating more bad food than good in my young days, but I make sure that inside be clean. Never over-eat. It's better to be a little hungry for man get sick when them eat too much.

I believe that people nowadays have to keep them inside clean more than how we use to because the food today is not good. As soon as them done cook, in no time the food nowadays get sour. We use to keep our food overnight and it hardly ever get sour. Whatever them put in them food, I don't know, but when it get sour that quickly, that means the food is no good.

To keep yourself clean outside, you can use lime and lime bush to clean the skin. When lime is scarce, use aloe. Whenever you don't feel satisfied with the smell of your mouth, just chew lime bush or clove to freshen up the breath. Peas bush and charcoal was our toothpaste and we also used to use a little light soda water to gargle the throat. The soda keeps the teeth hard and they don't get on edge too quickly.[4]

When you get hot and sweaty don't just jump into cold water. Make sure that you wet up your two legs first, for you can't cramp so easy if you do that.

I use to have to dabble in mud and dung. I always had the feeling that people catch worms from them two things. I was always afraid of worms, for worms use to give people fits. Some people would die. I use to cut my finger and toe nails close up so that nothing could hold under them. I also make sure that I was using my lime and clean my nails to keep me free from worms. Every now and then I also would boil the worm grass and drink it for three days.

Remember, man need a little luck to live. I was lucky. I could meet serious accidents, somebody could hurt me. But I was never sick, not even a headache or a little cough did I get. But I didn't use all them things I mention with the hope to live long. I did them just to keep healthy. And even though I took special care to make sure my body was always clean, I don't think that was all that make me never sick. I believe that the Heavenly Father was protecting me. Through Him, I did nothing that was

4. Wear down.

beyond human endurance.

Almost ever since I start to work with the Goodwins I was rearing cattle. I had a few when I call it a day at work and I went on to look[5] for them. Them keep me active, you see. Back in 1965, when I was eighty-eight, I fell down off my donkey. Now I don't think that anything min do me, but my two granddaughters — they was nursing at the hospital — them force me to go there. I spent a few days there, but I don't see the reason why they sent me there because that hospital didn't give me nothing.

After I got out my children got down on me and say that I must be done away with the cattle and them. I agree that I should do so and relax for the remainder of my days. But it took me quite some time to get use to not having nothing to do. I start to feel sick. I was feeling tired and me joints start to ache me, pains all over my body. At last I went to see a doctor. He examine me and say nothing wrong. Time pass and finally I got use to be at home. The pains, the aches and even the tiredness leave me at last. I used my time to visit my relatives all over the place.

By 1966, the leaders of the AT & LU was mopping up everything. Again they won all the elected seats on the Council. The labour government was well in the saddle by then. The planters was only in charge of the sugar. I think that the planters was of the belief that if the union leaders was in charge of the government, then the same people should also be in charge of sugar. At that time there was no more honeymoon for sugar and, for a fact, everybody know that since the slavery time, the planters, the government and sugar and them was always hand in hand, always together.

In 1967, Antigua got full home rule from England and as soon as that happen, the planters give up sugar and leave.

Wilfred Jacobs got to be the land's first black governor and V.C. Bird got to be the premier and the first black man to be the chief planter. Remember that he was already the union president. The first thing he went to do as chief planter was to cut into the wages of the workers. The money that he fight Moody

5. Take care of.

Stuart to pay them he went and slice in two. The rates under him in 1967 was lower than what the white planters have to pay in 1963. What a thing! The rest of the union officers couldn't say a thing. There wasn't even a squeak from the AT & LU. The premier was still the boss of the union.

Some time the same year the union kick some people out. Now that cause a quarrel between the union leaders and the people. The people him kick out start up a new union — the Worker's Union. The leaders of the old union began to fight those of the new uion. Competition start between unions and both union try to get support to survive.

The new sugar boss then start to punish a lot of people that wasn't in agreement with him. Me, the old man, didn't escape the wrath of the new chief planter and them. All my children was supporters of the Worker's Union. My grandchildren, too, start to take part in the brand-new union. That cause my pension to stop. The little that I was getting to keep me till the Lord ready for me was gone. My own union president refuse me my pension. I tell you, it was hard. I have worked for it for over seventy-two years, but the AT & LU was in the strong position. Very strong. They was the boss of the land and the union. If you don't agree with the government, you would sure get punishment in one way or the other, and when the government punish you it was the union, the same people. I am getting the pension from the Goodwins for some of the service I give to the estate, though, so I was still lucky.

Still and all, the people that were kick out wasn't afraid of the government. There was a long quarrel between the new union led by Malcolm Daniel and George Walter and the old union. But I got a shock when I hear that the Labour Government read the Riot Act[6] to them sometime in 1968. That was the last thing I ever think that they would dream of doing. I was ready to go to town to see what it was like, but the bus wasn't running on that day and my people refuse to take me to town. They was mad because the old man — at ninety-one years — want to go to see the riot. I wanted to see if the scene was like it was fifty years

6. A state of emergency in which the army and the police hold absolute powers.

before when Gov. Mereweather order the police to shoot down people. But nega people a rule them land now. The time is far different to what it was in my time. The young generations will give account of them.

I am very old now. I was born a long, long time ago. I'm not a hundred yet, I'm still nine years from it. I remember when my mother die at ninety-eight years that I was of the belief that I will make up the two years she fell short of.[7] God knows best. I am still strong. I feel good, I can see and hear just fine. Of course, I have a little rheumatic pains but that is expected. I know what's going on. Nothing is wrong with me other than I am old.

During my lifetime, not only generations of people pass, but there have been unthinkable changes in the land. It has been a long way from Gov. MacGregor in 1834 to Gov. Jacobs in 1967. I think that the leaders there now should have better sense of values, particular to the things that use to make up the life of the people long ago. The government don't keep up the cave at Cedar Grove. They let the people build houses on it instead. That cave was a wonderful thing. The people lived there before Columbus came. I think the government shouldn't have let it to be in ruin. And I would never think that the government would go and use bulldozer and pull down Boon's Chair. What a thing! It could have been great excitement for the people today.

Neither did I think that even if I live for two more hundred years that the government and the Moravians would let the Spring Gardens Seminary to go fade out. That place was the mother of the advanced education in this land so I hope that they will see fit to fix it up.

In my young days and even up to lately, anytime I would go in the city, I would make sure that I go and look at the big mahogany tree where my people was put on sale. Today it's all plucked up. Now this generation we have now nar[8] know that there the slave maket min they. The planters that should be

---

7. At the time he believed he would live to be one hundred years old. In fact, he was nearly one hundred and six when he died.
8. Young Antiguans don't know there was once a slave market at the big mahogany tree near the court house.

ashamed of all them do to negas when them see the tree never pluck it up. It was our government and black people that pluck up that tree.

I know too, that there's some things that never change. One thing that never change is that the land suffer drought badly. But the government went and close up all the springs and wells that give the people water all that time. Nearly all them ponds and guts are closed up now. Even General Spring is no more. Of course, them build the desalting plant, but that soon mash up too.

I have some more things I want the young generations to remember. Antigua never have soft grass of its own. It was the early planters that brought the soft grass here. If you really stop planting the soft grass, then only the hard grass will be here after a time. That hard grass can't help the animals in the dry season and neither can it keep the land from washing out when the rains fall. It is contouring and planting grass that will keep the land from washing out and make it green even when the drought is on.

The planters use to build a pond in every sugar cane field and put the crown of the King or Queen of England at the bottom of each pond. And those ponds was cleaned every year. So too was the channels that led to the ponds and guts. Pond weeds use to be planted in all them ponds to keep the sun from sucking out the water and there use to be trees around the important ponds and guts to shade the hot sun from the water. That was to make sure that the water last as long as possible. Them trees was also used to tie the soil and keep it from washing into the ponds. But almost all the ponds and dams that them have now is left wide open. It's a worry for me that this generation is going to suffer worse from drought than all the generations after Columbus.

If you fix up the water courses and keep them properly, I bet you the people will have plenty water. Man used to use fork and shovel and make them ponds and guts. Now the new machines is here to make it a little easier, but I don't see them closing them up. Just look at the hills, them clean and hard now. That's because they let them wash to the sea. I hope that the people will understand that the caring of the water channel and the contouring and the planting is the only things that can save us in the drought.

I have live my life well, despite the hard times. If there is any regrets I have, the only one throughout my long life is that I wasn't greedy. Or maybe it was that I was too honest. Maybe I worked too hard for the massas. And I think that I should've paid more attention to my children. I am proud of them. They learnt to work for themselves. None of them ever make me feel ashamed, thank God. I don't have any enemy. Not even one. In my young days a man with plenty of gals was called great and fruitful. Now them say a sin. Well if a so, my only sin is Woman. Well then, maybe no man commit more sins than me in that way. But God will forgive me.

I hope that you will write down exactly what I am telling you. If you do, the people will see how far down in the mud arwe come from. This generation will take care of what is happening to them. I hope that the day will never come again when our people have to suffer indignity like my generation and others have to. I am here to watch and see till the Lord take me home.

Postcript:

Samuel Smith, Papa Sammy to his family and friends, lived on, watching and seeing until December 6, 1982, twenty-six days short of his one hundred and sixth birthday.

His one hundredth birthday in 1977 brought his large family and many friends together for a big celebration, complete with visits from Gov. Sir Wilfred Jacobs, former Premier Goerge Walter, newspaper and radio reporters, and Connie Jacobs, the co-ordinator of Senior Citizens in Antigua.

The last three years of Papa Sammy's life were marked by visits to family and friends and tours of many of the places he talks about in this book. Throughout he kept up his daily exercise and was alert and interested in the world until the end. The last time we talked he said he was "a little shake, but the old man is making out".

Three days after this conversation, Papa Sammy died at home and was buried in the Methodist churchyard at Freeman's Ville. People from all over Antigua turned out to bid farewell to Freeman's Village first known centurian. One said Papa Sammy's funeral was so big because he was at peace with the people with whom he lived and worked. His son Hilson recalls, "My father struggled through the dark, dark days and he still outlived the many estate owners who used to be so powerful. Those of us whom he left behind can't help to be jealous of his strength, longevity, knowledge and his amazing photographic memory. Indeed, we hope that "plantin sucker will follow the root."

Early Folk Songs of Antigua

The folk songs of Antigua are a very important tool for Papa Sammy and his people to express their inner feelings. Every so often the grand old man would sing about the sad and bad times he and his people encountered. We present these very touching songs that are the expression of an oppressed people.

These songs, according to Papa Sammy, were not composed by any single individual but by individual groups such as prisoners and field workers. The songs deal with social and economic themes. This we believe is understandably so, since Papa Sammy and his people were forced to remain "one bite away from starvation".

It is obviously true that all the deadening monotony of life under slavery and colonialism cannot escape us, when we hear "we had to work like son of man".

Naturally then, the Antiguan working man knew what he had to face, any time he made an attempt to restructure the social and economic order of society. They would be beaten back in line with the "cat-o-nine tail".

We believe that the themes of these songs will help to clarify any doubts of the socio-economic exploitation Papa Sammy and his people encountered.

The songs are:

HARD WORK

We work till Jesus come
We work
Like son of man
We work
Till Jesus come
We work

A fork de land
We work
A cut de cane
We work
A dig de root
We work
A hold de bakkra plough
We work
A work till Jesus come
We work

A work like son of man
We work
We work till Jesus come
A work.

JERUSALEM MY HOPE

Jerusalem my happy home
When shall I go to see
Jerusalem my happy home
This place is not for me

Too much bread and water
This place is not for me
Too much hard labour
This place is not for me

Them lock up and walk with de key
This place is not for me
Woe, woe, Jerusalem, Jerusalem
I shall go to see.

SEND DOWN THE RAIN

The land is hard
The trees dying
Send down the rain

No water to drink
No food to eat
Send down the rain

No grass to weed
No plant to seed
Send down the rain

Massa harvest just too small
The people can't get it all
Send down the rain

Rain for the just
Rain for us
Send down the rain.

GOOD LORD YOU KNOW

Wa mek man must labour so
Good Lord you know
Sick or well a going ahead
Good Lord you know

A going till a drop down dead
Good Lord you know
Rain or sunshine de task a mine
Good Lord you know

Work for woman all day long
Good Lord you know
Working like the son of man
Good Lord you know.

KEEP ME FROM DYING

Let me tell de massa
Dem mus understand
We starving in this land
No bread, no cake, nothing to bite
We starving in this land
Just a bite keep me from
Starving, suffering
Just one bite from dying
Woe, woe, just one bite from dying

A look crab keep me from dying
A dig cackle keep me from dying
A look fish keep me from dying
A brock bakkra cane keep me from dying
Oh Lord, just one bite from dying
Woe, woe, one bite from dying.

CAT-O-NINE

They cover me face
So me can't see dem hit
I just want to know
The son of a bitch

Me can't complain
They cat me again
O Lord me fraid de cat-o-nine tail
Woe, woe, me fraid de cat-o-nine tail.

A Brief History of Antigua and Some Important Dates in Caribbean History

1493: Columbus departed from Cadiz, Spain on his second voyage and discovers Antigua, which he named Santa Maria de la Antigua, along with other islands in the Lesser Antilles and Jamaica. Spain claimed the sole right to navigate the Caribbean Sea, but largely ignores the smaller islands.

1506: The Spanish planted sugar cane in Santo Domingo, now the Dominican Republic.

1520: Spaniard Antonio Serrano was authorized to govern Antigua, Monsterrat, Barbuda, Dominica and Martinique and to people Guadelope, but "nunca hizo nada" — he never did anything.

1562: Englishman John Hawkins began the English slave trade.

1625: Under patent of the Great Seal of England, Antigua, St. Christopher, Nevis and Barbuda were taken under the protection of the British Crown.

1632: Englishman Sir Thomas Warner colonized Antigua and Monsterrat in the name of the British Crown.

1640
to
1647: Sugar industry was introduced into the Leeward Islands. Sugar became the main crop, the plantation or estate system flourished, black slavery became the order of the day.

1653: Caribs raided Antigua in effort to oust British colonists.

1663: British Crown formally granted Antigua to Lord Henry Willoughby who was named governor.

1666: The French navy raided Antigua.

1667: The Treaty of Breda between France and England made Antigua, Monsterrat and the English part of St. Christopher colonies of England.

1681: A hurricane devastated Antigua.

1696: Antigua became the seat of government for the British Leeward Islands.

1731: Severe drought in Antigua.

1736: Klass (Count) leads a failed slave revolt in Antigua.

1756: Moravian ministers sent to Antigua from England.

1760: Nathaniel Gilbert established the first Methodist Society in Antigua and the western hemisphere.

1768: Slaves in Monsterrat planned a revolt.

1776
to
1783: The U.S. War of Independence caused severe food shortages throughout the Leeward Islands.

1785: Runaway slaves and Caribs revolted in Dominica.

1789: Severe drought in Antigua. Toussaint and Dessalines led slave uprising in Haiti.

1800: Sometime between 1800 and the abolition of the slave trade in 1807 Mother Rachel, Samuel Smith's great-great grandmother, was seized on the west coast of Africa, enslaved and shipped in chains to Antigua.

1802: Haiti declared its independence.

1804: Severe drought in Antigua. In Barbados, one thousand negroes died before a rebellion was quelled.

1807: England abolished the slave trade, but slavery itself continued.

1834: Complete emancipation for Antiguan slaves. Mother Rachel and her daughters Fanny and Barba went in search of Minty, a daughter sold away during slavery. Fanny later gives birth to Countis, grandmother of Samuel Smith.

1841: Great fire struck Antigua.

1843: Severe earthquake hit Antigua. Most of the sugar works tumbled down and the cathedral was practically destroyed.

1844: Antigua's census returns listed 36,178 inhabitants.

1847: Fierce hurricane in Antigua causes 100,000 pounds sterling in damages.

1863: Steam plough began to be used in Antigua.

1865: St. Thomas uprising in Jamaica; George William Gordon and Paul Bogle executed.

1871: Hurricane hit Antigua.

1871 to 1874: Severe drought in Antigua; many estates cut back or completely stop production. Many labourers emigrated to Puerto Rico, Guadelope and Trinidad.

1877: Samuel Smith was born on New Year's Day.

1884: Heavy depression hit the sugar industry.

1891: Dredging of St. John's harbour was attempted in Antigua.

1897: Royal Commission began to investigate the crisis in the sugar industry and "the probable result of a complete failure of the sugar industry on the conditions of the labouring classes, both West Indian and East Indian . . ."

1899: Severe storm hit Antigua.

1900: Walling reservoir was completed in Antigua, with a capacity of 13,000,000 gallons.

1904: Central sugar factories opened at Gunthorpes and Bendals estates in Antigua; a law was also passed forbidding the practice of "certain vulgar frauds, commonly known as Obeah, and other pretended supernatural or occult practices in this colony (Antigua)."

1910: A Royal Commission met to inquire into the promotion and extension of trade between Canada and the West Indies.

1910 to 1912: Severe drought in Antigua; the Wallings Reservoir was almost empty and the supply system for St. John's practically a complete failure.

1911: Coconut industry began in Antigua and Nevis.

1914 to 1918: The First World War.

1917: Electric lights installed in a short stretch of St. John's, Antigua.

1918: Some estate owners in Antigua attempted to impose crop payment by weight instead of payment by row; cane workers strike; on March 9th, the government enforces the

Riot Act; a commission decided that payment for that year will be by the row.

1918: Renewed labour unrest in Antigua.

1924: Two hurricanes hit Antigua.

1928: Another hurricane hit Antigua.

1934: The one hundredth anniversary of the abolition of slavery. In the same year Portuguese businessmen built a rum distillery at Rat Island, Antigua. The gyrottiller plough is also introduced.

1936 to 1938: Popular discontent widespread in Barbados, Trinidad and Jamaica.

1938: Bustamante organized an industrial union in Jamaica.

1939: The Antigua Trades and Labour Union (AT & LU) was formed. World War II broke out in the same year.

1954: Samuel Smith became the oldest person in Freeman's Ville.

1957: Carnival was introduced in Antigua.

1962: Jamaica became the first British colony in the Caribbean to gain independence. It was followed in the same year by Trinidad and Tobago.

1966: Guyana and Barbados became independent.

1967: Formation of the Antigua Workers Union.

1967: Antigua gets full internal self-government from England. Sir Wilfred Jacobs became the first black governor of the island.

1968: Widespread labour unrest in Antigua. A general strike followed by a riot took place. The government enforced the Riot Act.

1981: Antigua became an independent nation.

1982: Samuel Smith died at the age of 105 after having lived twenty-three years in the 19th century and eighty-two in the 20th century.

The Family Tree of Samuel Smith

MOTHER RACHAEL: Speaks little English. Arrives in Antigua 1800 as a slave from Africa. Sold to Old Road estate slave owners. Has three daughters.

MINTY: Youngest child separated from the family and sold to Sanderson estate owners. Reunited after slavery ended.

BARBA: First daughter of Mother Rachael and an Antiguan born slave.

FANNY: Second child of Rachael. Was determined to unite the family after slavery ended.

COUNTIS: The first post-slavery baby. Grandmother of Samuel Smith, the person who told him about slavery.

DANIEL SMITH: Biological father of Samuel Smith. Common law husband of Margarette. He lived to be 78 years old.

MARGARETTE EDWARDS: First post-slave generation to go to school. She lived to be 98 years old.

SAMUEL SMITH: Born in 1877. Died in 1982. Raised by the daughter of a slave woman who informed him of his family roots.

This is the family tree of Samuel Smith. His ancestors came from Africa to Antigua as slaves nearly two hundred years ago.

About the Authors

KEITHLYN B. SMITH was born and raised in Antigua. He gained vast experience through his work as Secretary General of the Antigua Workers' Union. He served as a senator in the Parliament of Antigua, and is committed to social, economic and political well-being of working people.

FERNANDO C. SMITH was born and raised in Antigua and now lives in Toronto, Ontario, Canada.

He holds diplomas in accounting and business studies, and a bachelor of arts degree from York University. He is a member of the Antigua and Barbuda Association of Toronto.